SMART MONEY
DECISIONS

SMART MONEY DECISIONS

Why You Do What You Do with Money
(and how to change for the better)

MAX H. BAZERMAN

John Wiley & Sons, Inc.
New York • Chichester • Weinheim
Brisbane • Singapore • Toronto

This book is printed on acid-free paper. ☉

Copyright © 1999 by Max H. Bazerman. All rights reserved.

Published by John Wiley & Sons, Inc.
Published simultaneously in Canada.

Library of Congress Cataloging-in-Publication Data:

Bazerman, Max H.
   Smart money decisions : why you do what you do with money (and how to change for the better) / Max Bazerman.
      p.   cm.
   Includes index.
   ISBN 0-471-29611-2 (alk. paper)
   1. Finance, Personal.   2. Negotiation.   I. Title.
HG179.B347   1999
332.024—dc21   98-40652

Printed in the United States of America.

10 9 8 7 6 5 4 3 2

*To the many coauthors, students, clients, and friends
who have helped me think through the ideas
that appear in this book.*

PREFACE

During the past two decades, I have spent my professional career conducting research, writing books, teaching MBA students, training new faculty to teach at leading business schools, and doing consulting for many profit and nonprofit organizations. In these endeavors, I have focused on decision making and negotiation, research areas created to help people think more systematically about how to make wiser decisions to improve their lives and their company's performance. Specifically, my expertise is on the psychology of why we don't follow much of the wise advice that is easily available to us.

I have had the good fortune to work for many of the world's finest organizations, including McKinsey, Johnson & Johnson, IBM, Xerox, Lucent Technologies, Motorola, and The Nature Conservancy. However, much of what I know about decision making and negotiation comes from talking to friends about everyday decisions—buying and selling cars and houses, thinking through job offers, buying insurance, and so forth. These everyday decisions are the core of this book, which I have written for anyone who is interested in improving how he or she thinks about money.

The practical ideas offered in this book are based on sound research, which the interested reader can explore further with the aid of the citations provided in the endnotes. Many of the ideas in this book have been developed in conjunction with a number of fine colleagues. Among the many who have most directly influenced these ideas are Sally Blount, Jeanne Brett, Tina Diekmann, Don Jacobs, George Loewenstein, Beta Mannix, David Messick, Don Moore, Keith Murnighan, Ann Tenbrunsel, Leigh Thompson, Kathleen Valley, Marc Ventresca, and Kimberly Wade-Benzoni.

Since 1985, I have been a member of the Organization Behavior Department of the J. L. Kellogg Graduate School of Management at Northwestern University. I specifically appreciate the collegial and financial support of the Dispute Resolution Research Center at Northwestern University. The most important resource offered by Kellogg is a continuing stream of excellent colleagues who have helped to improve my thinking about the ideas in this book. I finished the final revisions on this book while serving as a visiting faculty member at the Harvard Business School, as well as a research affiliate at the Program on Negotiation at Harvard. The support of these institutions has been of significant value to me.

I have also benefited from my many arguments with Marla Felcher, my spouse. She is certainly the most vocal critic of how I think about money. Like many authors, I often draw on my own experiences. Thus, many of Marla's critiques of my money mistakes show up without citation throughout this book.

Finally, I have benefited significantly from an excellent research team that helped to develop the ideas in this book, provided writing and editorial assistance, and tested the logic of my arguments. This team included Amy Binder, Claire Buisseret, Leah Kidwell, and Alex Ooms. The book was also improved by useful feedback from Barry Nalebuff, Loretta Barrett (my agent), and Debby Englander (my editor at Wiley). Most central to the team has been my valued editor over the past seven years—Katie Shonk. Katie now knows more about decision making, negotiation, and personal finance than she ever aspired to know. More important, she brought to this book her wonderful writing skills, which make the reading of this book more enjoyable and beneficial. When Katie's novel eventually arrives, buy it—she is a wonderful writer.

MAX H. BAZERMAN

Evanston, Illinois, and
Cambridge, Massachusetts
July 1999

CONTENTS

Contents

SMART MONEY DECISIONS

1

DO I HEAR $5 FOR A $100 BILL?

One thing I have learned over the years as a professor and student of human behavior is that even very bright people make money decisions that cost them hundreds, thousands, and even millions of dollars. People waste money, and this bothers them! Furthermore, the money mistakes that they make are preventable—by improving the intuitive strategies they use when approaching their financial decisions.

To see the kind of money mistakes people make, consider the problem that I created for a group of executive students who were attending one of my lectures. I took a $100 bill from my wallet and announced the following:

> I am auctioning this $100 bill to the highest bidder. All members of the audience are free to participate or watch the bidding of others. Participants are welcome to bid in multiples of $5 until no further bidding occurs. The highest bidder pays the amount he or she bids for the $100. This auction differs from traditional auctions in that the

Katie Shonk and Leah Kidwell provided editorial assistance for this chapter.

second-highest bidder must also pay the last amount that he or she bid, although he or she will obviously not win the $100. For example, if Warren bids $15 and Charlene bids $20, and then the bidding stops, Charlene will pay me $20 for the $100 bill (earning an $80 profit), and Warren, the second-highest bidder, will pay me $15 and get nothing in return. Who will bid $5 to start the auction?

I have run this auction many times with undergraduate students, graduate students, and executives, and I have sold $1, $10, $20, and $100 bills. The pattern is always the same, regardless of how much money is at stake. The bidding starts out fast and furious until it reaches the $70–$80 range (on the $100 bill). Then, everyone except the two highest bidders drops out of the auction. The two bidders then begin to feel trapped. One bidder has bid $65 and the other $70. The $65 bidder must either bid $75 or give me $65 (and receive nothing in return). The uncertain option of bidding further (a choice that might produce a gain if the other bidder quits) seems more attractive than the sure loss, so the $65 bidder bids $75. This continues until the bids are $95 and $100.

Then, to everyone's surprise, the decision to bid $105 is very similar to all previous decisions. The $95 bidder can accept a $95 loss or continue and reduce his or her loss if the other bidder quits. Of course the rest of the group roars with laughter when the bidding goes over $100, which it usually does.

Obviously, the bidders are making money mistakes. But which bids are the mistakes? Twenty-dollar auctions typically end between $20 and $70. However, I have sold a $20 bill for $407, and I have had eleven $20 auctions hit the $100 mark. I once sold a $100 bill for $505. In total, I have earned over $20,000 running these auctions in classes over the last decade.[1]

This game, the dollar-auction, was first introduced by Martin Shubik.[2] I have adjusted the auction from $1 to other quantities to account for inflation and to make the auctions a bit more interesting. If you think about the auction, it would seem that participants who bid are caught in a money trap. It is true that one more bid may get the other party to quit. But when both bidders feel this way, the result can be catastrophic. Yet, without knowing the expected bidding patterns of the opponent, we cannot conclude that continued bidding is clearly wrong. What is the solution? Successful money management requires that you learn to identify money traps such as this one. The key to solving this problem lies in identifying the auction as a trap and, therefore, choosing not to make even a very small bid.

Another approach is to develop strategies that discourage your competitors from bidding. Think about what you would do, now that you know the rules and the trap that exists. If a class knew that an auction was coming, one class member could organize the group to collude against the speaker. If one person bid $5, and everyone else refrained from bidding, the class could later divide the $95 profit. Communication can be a very effective tool.

In the $100 auction, it is easy to see three money mistakes in action. First, bidders enter the auction as a result of the *failure to consider the decisions of other parties.* Imagine that you bid $20 after someone else bids $15, and no one new comes in at $25. What will the $15 bidder do, quit and lose $15 or bid $25? The $15 bidder will bid $25, and you will bid $30. The $25 bidder will bid $35, and this logic will take the bidding up to $95 and $100. The key to avoiding this trap is to consider the decisions of the other bidder. The only event that saves any bidder from a monetary loss is the emergence of a new bidder who substitutes himself into the trap, which only brings the original bidder back to a breakeven point.

Now I also mentioned that bids often exceed $100 (or $20 in a $20 auction). Why? Because most $95 bidders would rather *escalate their commitment* to the auction rather than accept the loss. They feel that they are already "knee deep in the big muddy."[3] Similarly, the $100 bidder may very well escalate his or her bid to $110 rather than accept the $100 loss. The tendency to escalate commitment to a previous course of action is a pervasive money mistake.

Yet what accounts for two bidders passing the $100 mark on a $20 auction? My experience is that bidders often forget their objectives, *wanting to beat the other party* no matter what the cost. They are motivated to win the auction rather than to make a profitable decision. This is consistent with how egos can affect bidding wars in the corporate context.

The $100 auction closely mirrors a scenario that occurred in late 1995 between American Airlines, United Airlines, and USAir (now USAirways). USAir, the nation's fifth largest airline, announced that it was for sale at the right price. Wall Street analysts speculated that the two industry leaders, United and American, were the most obvious bidders. These analyses, however, were limited to the expectation that the value of USAir was higher to United or American than as a stand-alone company.

These analyses failed to consider that United and American would be extremely motivated to avoid the loss of a bidding war, since USAir joining American would create a major market positioning setback to United, and USAir joining United would create a similar major loss to American. In fact, the loss to United if American made the acquisition would be larger than the gain obtained by American. Similarly, the loss to American if United made the acquisition would be larger than the gain obtained by United. These are perfect conditions for a dysfunctional bidding war to emerge. Neither side can afford to allow the other party to win. As American or United, what would you do?

Robert Crandall, the chairperson of American, developed a strategy to preempt a money mistake. He wrote a letter to the 118,000 employees of American Airlines stating that American would "increase its size and reach . . . by internal growth—not by consolidation." Crandall went on to state that American would "not be the first to make a bid for USAir," but would "be prepared to respond with a bid" or take another line of action if United tried to acquire USAir.[4] While the letter was addressed to American Airline employees, its most important target was obviously United. Crandall was sending a message: keep things as they are, or we will both end up in a money-losing bidding war. Crandall's letter was very effective in avoiding the three money mistakes listed above in an industry known for dysfunctional competition.

A Framework for Avoiding Money Mistakes

The mistakes just discussed (and many more) are easy to understand, largely because of fascinating research in cognitive psychology. The psychological study of how we make decisions provides a great deal of insight into our money mistakes. Rather than offering a simplistic multistep process for making wiser decisions, this book provides an opportunity to audit how you think about money. Each chapter of *Smart Money Decisions* introduces a common real-world dilemma, describes the errors that people too often make in this situation, explains the psychology behind these mistakes, and offers advice on how to avoid making them in the future.

This book spotlights the most common and most important mistakes people make with their money and their lives. Readers should recognize themselves in each chapter as I identify the common missteps people take in a variety of real-world situations such as buying a house, investing money, and making career decisions.

This book views readers as intelligent people who have been successful, but whose decisions are biased in ways that seriously compromise their potential. Readers will see how habit has forced them into a set of hard-to-break cognitive procedures, imposing constraints on their monetary decisions. This book will both challenge and annoy readers as they think about many of their own money mistakes. But most importantly, this book will help readers identify mistakes they currently make that can be corrected.

Many books on personal finance tell you how to make wise decisions. Although these books often provide good advice, many people fail to correct their mistakes after reading them. Why? Most books and magazines offering advice on money fail to give readers an essential understanding of how to change their behavior. An awareness of one's imperfections is not sufficient. For example, knowing that you are a bad cook, poor investor, or wasteful consumer is not enough to remedy the problem. In order to change your monetary behaviors (or any of these other problematic behaviors), you must (1) "unfreeze" existing decision patterns, (2) understand the changes necessary for making better decisions, and (3) create the conditions that allow you to "refreeze" better ideas.[5] Applying this model of change, the book guides you through these three basic steps with the goal of permanently improving your monetary decisions.

Unfreezing

In order for change to occur and last over time, an unfreezing process must take place. Because people have used their intuitive strategies for many years, changing these patterns is psychologically disturbing. An individual may not like learning that he or she is a bad decision maker, particularly when this entails recognizing lost resources and missed opportunities in the past. To admit that there is something fundamentally wrong with our decision-making processes is inconsistent with our concepts of ourselves as successful money managers. Believing that one is an excellent decision maker is a much more comfortable mindset and, therefore, likely to dominate without a concerted effort to change. To combat this resistance, this book provides real stories to motivate you, confronts the psychology behind common money mistakes, and provides guidance to counteract the dysfunctional aspects of our intuition.

Change

Once you are unfrozen from past behaviors, a willingness to consider alternatives develops. Change, however, is far from guaranteed; the individual is likely to resist and continually reassess the desirability of change. There are three critical steps in the process of changing financial decision-making processes: (1) identification of specific money mistakes; (2) explanation of the roots of these mistakes; and (3) reassurance that these mistakes are not a challenge to your general intelligence. The first step involves identifying the key points of the concrete examples that the book uses for unfreezing. In addition, for the bias to have relevance to the individual, an explanation of why the bias exists is necessary. It is critical that the reader understand that virtually everyone has biases and that having them does not imply that one is a poor decision maker, only that one is human and therefore room for improvement exists.

Refreezing

Once the change takes place, it's still easy for the individual to revert back to past practices. New procedures are foreign and must develop into intuitive strategies. You need to consciously and diligently use the new knowledge in multiple applications until the new strategies become second nature, taking the place of old practices as intuitive strategies. My past students and readers of my earlier books have been very successful at refreezing new cognitive strategies, probably because people tend to continue behaviors that pay off. However, frequent application and repeat training are necessary if change is to last and become an established part of the individual's behavioral repertoire.

This model of change provides the structure of this book. In each chapter, I attempt to unfreeze your present monetary decision patterns by demonstrating your money mistakes, outlining better ways of thinking about specific decision problems, and discussing methods that you can use to refreeze your thinking to ensure that the changes will last.

Top 10 Money Mistakes

As you read this book and audit your own monetary decisions, you will discover patterns of financial errors. In my opinion, these are the 10 most important money mistakes that we make.

1. Overconfidence. Despite the other mental foibles listed here and throughout this book, most people are dramatically overconfident in their decision making. Overconfidence is the engine that allows all of these other money mistakes to operate unchecked. The entire book is designed not only to improve your decision making, but also to help you understand when you often place undeserved confidence in your intuition.

2. Being Unprepared. A common and fatalistic belief is that *either you've got it or you don't*. As a result, people ignore the benefits of thorough preparation in negotiation. Too many people "wing it" in important negotiations and make mistakes that could easily have been avoided. People assume that all the action occurs at the table, whereas in fact much of the important activity happens before the formal proceedings begin. Chapters 2, 3, and 4 show the importance of doing your homework.

3. Ignoring the Cognitions of Others. So much information would become available to us if we would only think about the decisions of other people. Yet we are not very good at putting ourselves in another person's shoes. The high bidders in the $100 auction are victims of this error. Chapter 9 examines this money mistake in negotiations, and Chapter 13 shows how it leads people to overpay in auctions.

4. Mythical Fixed Pie. If I win, then you have to lose. This belief is an unfortunate and false model of most negotiation problems. It is also the common psychological barrier to finding mutually beneficial trade-offs. Chapter 12 develops this money mistake in personal and business contexts and outlines clear strategies to bust the mythical fixed pie.

5. Overweighting Momentary Impulses. I want it now! Frequently we make decisions based on fleeting momentary impulses that contradict our long-term interests. As a result, people engage in a variety of dysfunctional behaviors (such as smoking and running up high credit card debt) that cause them to wonder, "What was I thinking?" a week later. Yet at the same time, ignoring what you want would make life boring. Chapter 7 examines the need to manage the conflict between what you want versus what you think you should do.

6. Anchoring. You receive a low offer on your house and respond with a counter. What did you just do? You accepted the low offer as a reasonable starting point for the negotiation. Frequently, an early number in a negotiation anchors our decision without our awareness. We see how this occurs in the context of buying a house in Chapter 2.

7. Escalation. Knee deep in the big muddy, throwing good money after bad, and entrapment are just a few of the terms that have been used to describe the psychological tendency to escalate commitment to a previous course of action. Developing this argument from the $100 auction, Chapter 10 examines this mistake and what you can do to avoid it in the future.

8. Focusing on Beating the Other Side. One of our most common instincts is to want to beat our opponent. Based on our earlier competitions, we inappropriately focus on our desire to win, rather than on making a good decision for ourselves. As a result, people getting divorced give too much of their assets to lawyers, and companies lose too much profit to dysfunctional competition. We saw this money mistake above in the $100 auction, and we examine it in detail in Chapter 9.

9. Ignoring Your Alternatives. Power in negotiation comes from your alternatives. Your willingness to buy a different house, a different car, or a different company increases your power at the negotiation table. Yet most negotiators go into many of the most important negotiations of their lives without thinking about their alternatives. Falling in love with three (houses, cars, companies, etc.) rather than with one can be a very effective negotiation strategy. We see this theme emerge when we discuss buying a house in Chapter 2 and buying a car in Chapter 3.

10. Falling for Vivid Scares. Remember that top-of-the-line car or stereo you bought after reading rave reviews about its high performance in *Consumer Reports*? Despite your confidence that you were buying a reliable brand, the salesperson convinced you to buy an overpriced warranty anyway. How did they do it? They helped you imagine the disaster that might occur if you passed on the warranty. Vivid scares are a central theme of your visit to the car dealership in Chapter 3 and your insurance purchase decisions in Chapter 4.

These top 10 money mistakes are the most important of the 24 more specific money mistakes described in this book. Avoiding each one can save you thousands of dollars. I summarize the complete list in the final chapter.

The 24 money mistakes do not define the chapter titles. Rather, these mistakes show up as we explore a variety of real-world money domains that I have selected based on their relevance to most people. They include the following: *buying and selling houses* (Chapters 2 and 9), *buying cars* (Chapters 3, 4, 5, and 9), *insurance decisions* (Chapters 3 and 4), *purchases in general* (Chapters 4, 5, 7, and 14), *investments* (Chapters 5, 6, 10, and 14), *auctions* (Chapters 1 and 13), *careers* (Chapters 7, 8, and 14), *marriage* (Chapters 11 and 12), and *competition* (Chapters 11 and 12).

I hope this book serves as a useful audit that provides a springboard to help you make more reasoned monetary decisions. Eliminating money mistakes will lead to greater financial security and can diminish or eliminate the regret that you typically experience after making a money mistake.

2

FALLING IN LOVE WITH ONE RATHER THAN THREE, AND OTHER COMMON HOUSE-BUYING MISTAKES

"I think I'm about to buy my dream house!" my friend Tina said exuberantly when I picked up the phone on a recent Sunday night.

"Wow, that was quick," I said. "You mentioned to me that you were about to start looking, but I didn't think you'd be at the buying stage already." Tina works for a well-known consulting firm, and just a week ago she told me that she was ready to upgrade from the condo she had bought back when she was a struggling entrepreneur.

"Well, I thought that I would go about this process cautiously, and trudge through open houses for months and months, but I really lucked out. I saw a house this afternoon—only the third one I've looked at—and it is absolutely perfect! It's a four-bedroom Victorian, just two blocks from the lake. It's been completely renovated,

Katie Shonk played a central role in the research and editing of this chapter, and Leah Kidwell provided editing assistance.

and it even has a Jacuzzi! Max, I am in love with this house, and I need your negotiation advice on how to snare it."

"I'd be happy to help. What exactly is the situation?" The excitement in Tina's voice made me very nervous. Since open houses are often held on Sundays, I frequently receive calls on Sunday nights from friends seeking advice on buying a house. Based on other Sunday night phone calls, I guessed that soon I would be forced into an awkward situation.

"Okay, here's the deal. The house's list price is $425,000. So right away I offered $360,000, and the seller immediately countered at $400,000. It all happened so fast! I told my broker that I was thrilled that I already saved $25,000 with my low initial offer. Isn't that great?"

"Um . . . well, why don't you tell me what happened next," I said uneasily.

"Well, my broker recommended that I move up significantly in price so that I wouldn't risk losing the house. But I told him that I had to call you first to determine my strategy."

"Gee, Tina, I'm flattered," I said, grimacing.

"Max, I can afford this great house and don't want to risk losing it, but I want to get a good deal. I need your advice on how to get the best price possible. What should my next move be?"

"Before we start talking strategy, Tina, I just want to make sure we both understand that buying a house is a particularly tricky negotiation. I hope our friendship won't suffer if things don't go exactly as you had hoped."

"Well, okay . . . but is there some reason you think I won't be happy with the result of this negotiation? Do you think I've already done something wrong?"

I stared at the floor and tried to think of a tactful way to tell Tina that she had already made several big, possibly irrecoverable mistakes in the opening hours of her negotiation.

I dislike these Sunday night phone calls. They are inevitably a no-win situation for me. If my advice leads to a higher closing price than my friend had hoped for, then she will be unimpressed with my expertise. If my advice causes my friend to lose the house to another buyer, she will be mad at me—especially if she has already indicated that she thought the house was wonderful. Unfortunately, getting the lowest price possible often requires running some risk of losing the house to another buyer. Any strategy other than accepting the other party's offer incurs some risk of impasse.

The frustrating aspect of such phone calls is that by the time my friends call me for advice on their real estate deals, they have already committed significant money mistakes. For many people, buying a house is the biggest monetary decision they will make in a decade, or even longer. Nevertheless, they often make unnecessary errors. In the scenario, my friend Tina has already committed three key mistakes:

1. She is not thinking about negotiation alternatives; she fell in love with the Victorian house after only seeing three houses and made an offer without having any other prospects.
2. She has anchored on the listing price; she took the $425,000 price too seriously.
3. She has told too much to her real estate broker; she forgot that realtors have their own agendas.

These three mistakes form the focus of this chapter.

Falling in Love with Three Rather Than One

What advice can I give to my friend? If I were willing to be blunt, I would tell her that she has already violated the most important rule of buying houses (or any other important negotiation, with the possible exception of mate selection)—*"fall in love with three, not just with one."* For the buyer to make a well-informed decision, she must first think about what would happen if she did not buy this house. How attractive is the next best option? Once you fall in love with a particular house and believe that you *have* to have it, your bargaining position is weakened. Falling in love with one house (or car or job) prevents you from thinking clearly and rationally about your best alternative and reduces your negotiation advantage. However, to the extent that you are willing to make an offer on an alternative house, you are better able to take the chance of losing the first house and waiting for the other party to concede. By realizing that you have an alternative to this particular negotiation, you strengthen your position in this and any future negotiations.

But when I give this advice to home buyers, they are blinded by love. They tell me, as patiently as they can, that they don't want a strategy for buying a *different* house; they want *this* house, their dream house. This is exactly my point, I tell them. Buyers typically search for a house by looking until they fall in love with one, and then they negotiate. However, your willingness to entertain the possibility of buying another house strengthens your bargaining position. In a typical housing market, is it more fun to be a buyer or a seller? Most people answer "buyer." Why? Because buyers have more options! Options provide power. Once a buyer falls in love with one house—and has to have it—their power has eroded to the level of the seller.

Setting Limits—Based on Knowing Your Alternative

Before you begin any important negotiation, you should consider the potential outcomes in the event that no agreement is reached. In other words, what is your **Best Alternative To** a

Negotiated Agreement (BATNA)?[1] In house buying, the most common BATNA is to buy a different house instead. This is much easier if you fell in love with three, rather than with just one. Thinking about your alternative is critical because the quality of this alternative allows you to think carefully about the upper bound for a negotiated agreement. If you cannot reach agreement, you will receive your BATNA. Thus, you should prefer any negotiated agreement that provides more value than your BATNA, in comparison to an impasse.

People enter into negotiations with a general target or at least some idea of what they want, yet most negotiators fail to specifically establish their reservation price or discover that of their opponent. A negotiator's reservation price is the point at which a negotiator is indifferent to the choice of a negotiated agreement or an impasse. A reservation price is closely related to the negotiator's BATNA. For example, if Tina doesn't buy this house, what house is she likely to buy instead? At what difference in price would Tina prefer the alternative house? Yes, Tina wants the Victorian house, but saving money by buying a less expensive house will allow her to spend money on a new kitchen, a cottage in the woods, a vacation, or a new car. Thus, establishing a BATNA means more than just considering a different house. Rather, it encompasses the entire package of what you will do if you do not buy this house. Buyers are often more open to thinking about another house once they consider what they could do with an extra $30,000.

By establishing and thinking about your BATNA, you can rationally assess the highest price that you are willing to pay before you would prefer to not reach an agreement. It's comforting knowing your BATNA. If the other party rejects an offer near the value of your BATNA, there's no reason for you to feel bad about reaching an impasse. You know that the amount of concession that would have been necessary to reach an agreement would have been unacceptable to you. Remember, the goal of negotiating is not to reach just any agreement, but rather to reach an agreement that is more desirable than what you would get without an agreement. While it is rare for negotiators to think about their BATNA, it is even rarer for individuals to think about their opponent's BATNA. However, by considering the other party's circumstances and likely alternative to a negotiated agreement, we can often get a wealth of information about how far they will budge before they will actually walk away from the negotiating table. The seller of a house who has already purchased another house will act very differently than someone who is just testing the residential market. This information may give a potential buyer a distinct advantage. One critical reason for paying attention to the alternatives of the other party is to be able to predict their level of rigidity in the negotiation. Unfortunately, it is sometimes quite difficult to assess the other party's alternative. However, whether the negotiator and his or her opponent have easy-to-assess reservation prices, or if the next best alternatives are more like comparing apples and oranges, the negotiator should always determine his or her BATNA and the best estimate of the value of an opponent's BATNA.

Bargain Hunting

In order to help organize this analysis of getting a good price on a house, I encourage buyers to think about their *bargaining zone*. The bargaining zone is the set of prices for which both the buyer and seller prefer agreement over impasse. Figure 2.1 is a diagrammatic analysis of Tina's house negotiation.

It is important to realize that the parties may have overly optimistic assessments of what they can get out of the negotiations. Unrealistic expectations will not serve you well because they will lead you to hold out for more than you can get.

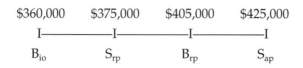

B_{io} = The buyer's initial offer—the price at which the buyer would be delighted to purchase the house.

S_{rp} = The seller's reservation price—the lowest price the seller would accept before walking out on the deal. At this point, the seller is indifferent between an agreement and an impasse.

B_{rp} = The buyer's reservation price—the highest price the buyer would accept before walking out on the deal. At this point, the buyer is indifferent between an agreement and an impasse.

S_{ap} = The seller's asking price—the seller would be delighted to receive this amount.

FIGURE 2.1 The bargaining zone.

Thinking wisely about the bargaining zone is a more useful strategy.

If Tina could accurately assess the likely bargaining zone, she could convince the seller of the Victorian house to accept $376,000 since this figure is above the seller's reservation price. However, it is also true that if the seller could convince Tina that $400,000 was the lowest amount that he or she would accept, Tina would probably agree to that price.

The conclusion we can draw from this analysis is that there is a wide range of settlements that would make both parties better off than reaching no agreement or an impasse. Yet impasses do occur, even when the alternative is the loss of the entire bargaining zone. Thinking rationally increases your chances of reaching an agreement that is beneficial for you.

Anchoring on the Listing Price

Tina appears to have assumed that the $425,000 list price of the house is an important signal. In fact, she considers any discount from the list price to be a gain. But what if the $425,000 price was way too high? Many house buyers measure their success by the reduction that they obtain off the list price. On the other hand, I argue that you should compare what you paid versus what the house is worth.

Tragically, people are affected by anchors without even realizing the effect of these anchors. In one study, people were asked to estimate the percentage of African countries in the United Nations.[2] For each subject, a *random* number (obtained by an observed spin of a roulette wheel) was given as a starting point. Subjects were then asked to state whether the actual percentage was higher or lower than this random number and then develop their best estimate for the actual percentage. Even the arbitrary numbers from the roulette wheel had a substantial impact on estimates. For groups that received 10 countries and 65 countries as random starting figures, their median estimates were 25 and 45, respectively. Thus, even though the people were aware that the anchor was random and unrelated to the judgment task, the anchor had a dramatic effect on their estimate.

Salary negotiations represent a very common context for observing anchoring as a money mistake. A specific company might have an average raise of 6 percent, with increases for specific employees varying from 2–10 percent. Society has led us to accept such systems as equitable. However, such a system falls victim to anchoring and leads to substantial inequities. What happens if an employee has been substantially underpaid to begin with? The pay system described does not rectify past inequities, since even a large increase will probably still keep that employee underpaid. Conversely, the system would work in the employee's favor, had he or she been overpaid.

Back to buying a house. Securing the cooperation of a real estate agent who had just put a house on the market, researchers Greg Northcraft and Margaret Neale spoke with a number of real estate agents to determine what type of information they used in valuing a piece of residential real estate.[3] They also asked the agents to provide an estimate of how accurately agents, such as themselves, could appraise the value of residential real estate. The real estate agents reported that any deviation from the appraisal value of more than 5 percent would be highly unusual and easily recognizable by the agents.

The researchers created a 10-page packet of information for the agents that included: (1) the standard Multiple Listing Service (MLS) listing sheet for the property; (2) a copy of the MLS summary of residential real estate sales for both the entire city and the immediate neighborhood of the house for the past six months; (3) information (including listing price, square footage, characteristics of the property, etc.) about other properties located in the same neighborhood divided into four categories—property currently for sale, property recently sold, property sold but the sale not complete, and property previously listed that did not sell; and (4) standard MLS listing information for other properties in the immediate neighborhood currently for sale. The researchers divided up the packets into four groups and changed two pieces of information in each of the groups—the asking price and the price per square foot if the asking price was paid. After having the property independently valued by three appraisers, the researchers took the average value of the appraisers and then set four different listing prices, which included a figure that was 12 percent higher than the appraised value, one that was 4 percent higher, one that was 4 percent lower, and one that was 12 percent lower than the appraised value. The researchers also changed the price per square foot to correctly reflect the listing price.

The agents came to evaluate the house in the normal course of their jobs. The researchers gave them one of the four packets of information and asked them to estimate the following:

1. The appraised value of the house.
2. An appropriate listing price for the house.
3. A reasonable price to pay for the house.
4. The lowest offer they would accept if they were the seller.

In addition, the researchers asked them to identify from a list the relevant considerations that had gone into their evaluation of this property as well as to give a brief description of the process they used to arrive at the four figures we requested.

Analyzing the data from these real estate agents provided some very interesting results. The listing price provided to the real estate agents had a major impact on their valuation process; they were more likely to have high estimates on all four prices when the listing price was high than when the listing price was low. When the researchers tried to figure out what information the agents thought they were using, another interesting pattern emerged. Although it is clear that listing price played a big role in the agents' evaluation of the worth of the house, only 19 percent of the agents mentioned listing price as a factor they considered, and only 8 percent indicated listing price as one of their top three considerations. Interestingly, almost three-quarters of the agents reported using a computational strategy in assessing the value of the real estate. To determine the value of the property, 72 percent of the agents indicated that they took the average price per square foot of houses that had recently sold (the comparables), multiplied that number by the number of square feet in the property, and then adjusted for the condition of the house. If they had indeed implemented such a strategy, then we could not have observed the anchoring effect of the listing price. With that strategy, the listing price would have been irrelevant. The conclusion: Initial offers critically influence the perceived parameters of the negotiation.

Final agreements are more strongly influenced by initial offers than by subsequent counteroffers. Since issues under consideration in the negotiation may be of uncertain or ambiguous value, an initial offer can anchor the subsequent concessions of both parties. Once negotiators respond to these initial offers with suggested adjustments, the anchor of the initial offer has achieved some measure of credibility. If an initial offer is too extreme, the negotiator must reanchor the process, even if this means threatening to walk away from the table rather than agreeing to an unacceptable starting point for the negotiation.

Where Do Listing Prices Come From?

If the seller is using a real estate agent, he or she faces the task of choosing an agent to handle the sale. One way to accomplish this is to have a number of agents evaluate the property and propose a listing price to the owner. If the owner is given a series of options, which option is he or she most likely to accept? Probably the one from the agent that suggests the highest listing price. Assuming this is true, we can predict the behavior of the typical agent. He or she will obviously suggest a high listing price in order to secure the account.

Once set, the listing price quickly becomes an anchor for the owner in evaluating subsequent offers. The listing price has been systematically overstated—unbeknownst to the seller, who anchors at this relatively extreme point and thus rejects offers that may, in fact, represent fair offers for the property. If the seller does not adjust sufficiently from the agent's extreme anchor, then the house remains on the market unsold for a much longer period of time than it would have if the seller were more realistically anchored.

The listing price of a piece of real estate is the initial offer made by the seller in potential negotiations over the purchase of the property. This anchors one end of the negotiation—the target of the seller; that is, the seller is very happy to be offered the listing price as the selling price for the property. The listing price is an optimistic goal set by the seller (often in consultation with the real estate agent) for what it is he or she wants to achieve in the negotiation. Realistically, however, most sellers expect to get something less than the listing price for their homes and adjust downward from their optimistic goal. However, the adjustments that sellers typically make from the listing price are simply insufficient. The seller then incurs costs from this anchoring-and-insufficient-adjustment process; he or she is unable to sell the house or has the house on the market much longer than should have been the case had a more rational assessment been conducted.

When my friends Claire and Tom asked me for advice on selling their house *before* they put it on the market, I gladly coached them on BATNA, reservation prices, and anchoring-and-adjustment. Assisted by a real estate agent, Claire and Tom posted a listing price of $650,000 on their house, a figure they considered to be high, but not outrageous. My friends received an initial offer of $500,000. Being strongly motivated to complete the deal, Claire and Tom countered with $600,000, and the buyer returned with $550,000. Claire and Tom knew that they would not go below their reservation price of $580,000, yet sensed that the negotiation was anchored to head in that direction. At a meeting with the buyer, Claire and Tom pleasantly explained that $550,000 would be unacceptable to them, and, furthermore, that $575,000 was as well. Claire and Tom reiterated their $600,000 offer, and emphasized their willingness to be flexible on financing, furniture, and so forth. Their goal was to move the anchor to $600,000, even if an adjustment was necessary. The response was a set of minor adjustments from the new anchor of $600,000. Claire and Tom's reanchoring proved successful, and best of all, for me, our friendship wasn't jeopardized by any awkward Sunday evening phone calls.

The Agent: Trusted Advisor or Parasitic Intermediary?

"I told my broker that I was thrilled that I already saved $25,000 with my low initial offer," Tina told me in our phone conversation. I was dismayed to hear what she had revealed to her agent; in fact, I am often shocked when I hear what people tell their real estate agents. They treat this person as a confidant, a trusted advisor, and a source of negotiation inspiration. In fact, the agent is a third party in the negotiation with his or her own set of interests and concerns.

It is critical to understand the logical role of the agent in the real estate negotiation process. Agents exist in many situations because of their specialized knowledge. Agents are those who act for, on behalf of, or as representatives of the disputants or principals. Because of their specialized knowledge of the housing market, real estate agents identify and match prospective buyers and sellers. In some cases, the agent may be passive, simply acting as a messenger who transmits information between the principals. In others, the agent may take a more active role, directly participating in the fashioning of an agreement. The agent receives a percentage of the selling price from the seller. As such, the realization that the agent's incentive structure does not match the desires of *both* the buyer and seller simultaneously is critical to understanding this negotiation process.

Whatever the agent receives from the transaction must come from one or both of the parties. Thus, the joint surplus available in a direct negotiation between the buyer and seller will be reduced when negotiating through an agent. In a residential real-estate setting, the potential buyer and seller depend on the real estate agent(s) to represent them. The agent typically is legally responsible only to the seller, regardless of the agent-buyer relationship, since it is the seller who pays the commission (usually 5–7 percent of the selling price). Given that the agent receives a commission based on the selling price, the agent has a clear incentive to be biased in the direction of the seller's interests. The structure of this interest may influence both the transmitting and presenting of information in the negotiation process. However, the most important incentive of the agent is to close the deal.

Who Really Pays for the Agent?

The use of an agent is expected to increase the sales price of a piece of property, since the seller pays the agent's commission out of the surplus created by the sale. However, the amount of the increase is unclear. One viable prediction is that the selling price will increase (at least) by the amount of the agent's commission. When assured of an agreement, the agent routinely has an incentive to increase the selling price of the property. This could push the price beyond the point where the additional surplus covers the commission. Such an argument is commonly used by realtors when trying to convince a seller to list with an agent rather than attempting to sell a home without one.

In contrast, when individuals or professional appraisers evaluate the market value of a home, they do not provide one figure for its value if sold by an agent and another figure for its value if sold without an agent. Rather, market value implies the objective value of a property, regardless of the mechanism by which that property is transmitted from seller to buyer. The value (and subsequently the price) of the property should not change as a result of the agent's involvement. These two perspectives on agents lead to very different conclusions. The first suggests that the buyer ends up paying the agent's commission; the second suggests that the seller incurs this cost. In one study of actual real estate negotiations, it was concluded that sellers and buyers roughly split the cost of the realtor's commission.[4]

What to Tell Your Agent: Mum's the Word

My colleagues and I examined the impact of an agent's knowledge of the buyer's and/or seller's reservation points in a residential real estate negotiation.[5] We considered the impact on selling price, percent of an agent's commission, and impasse rate when four different conditions of knowledge existed: (1) the agent did not know the buyer's or the seller's reservation points; (2) the agent knew the buyer's reservation point, but not the seller's; (3) the agent knew the seller's reservation point, but not the buyer's; and (4) the agent knew both the buyer's and seller's reservation points. We found that the selling price was lowest when the agent knew only the seller's reservation price. When the agent knew only the buyer's reservation point, the agent took advantage of this knowledge and the final selling price was the highest of the four in this condition. The highest agent fee, both in dollars and percentage of sale price, occurred in the buyer-knowledge condition, while the highest impasse rate occurred in the know-both condition.

This section highlights the importance of considering the decision-making processes and incentive structures of agents. Negotiators can maximize their interests if they rationally consider all the available information concerning each party at the table—not just the disputants. The agent should be considered a party to the dispute with his or her own set of interests. Thus, you should only provide the agent with information that will be in the agent's best interest to use in your interest. Generally, this means that you should not tell the agent anything that you would not tell the other side.

Agents are not evil, but they are people who often have different interests than the principle negotiators. Agents can provide a wealth of information, handle many of the details of the transaction process, and orient you to a new area. In fact, the structure of the residential real estate market creates a context in which it is a mistake to try to buy a house without an agent. The problems occur when you also expect them to be your unbiased negotiation advisor. This is an unreasonable expectation!

Advice

It is possible, and relatively easy, to avoid the most common mistakes people make when negotiating for one of their most important purchases—their house. In summary, these are the three steps you should follow:

1. Imagine what you will do if you do not buy the dream house you have your eye on. Thinking about your options provides another source of power.

2. Use anchoring to your advantage by setting realistic, yet favorable, goals. If you are too extreme, no one will pay attention to your price. If you are too concessionary, the target will be set too low.

3. Realize that the agent's job is to close the deal, not to protect your interests. It isn't reasonable to expect the agent to act against his or her interests in order to protect you economically. That's your job. Think of the agent as another party at the negotiation table, not as your buddy.

Keep in mind that the recommendations in this chapter can be applied to all of the important negotiations in your life.

Chapter

3

I Got the Car for Less Than Invoice

*O*ne Saturday afternoon, when the game on TV is pretty much decided by the third quarter, Henry wanders into the car dealership near his house. He has been thinking about buying a car for a few months, and he's talked to some of his friends and knows a few models he wants to check out. As soon as Henry enters the front door of the car dealership, he begins to feel overwhelmed. He can't find a salesperson who is free, so he searches through a maze of new models, all of them with features he doesn't quite understand (and doesn't think he cares about). He finds the model he read about in the newspaper, but also pauses at some with which he is less familiar. He realizes he has little understanding, other than the basic factor of size, of why one model is a few thousand dollars more than another.

As Henry tries to decide whether he really needs rear-wheel suspension or air-cooled injection, a salesperson silently appears at his shoulder. Henry is desperate for some guidance. There are all sorts of models and options he has never considered, and how is he supposed to know what any of these cars are actually worth? So he

Alex Ooms played a central role in the research and writing of this chapter. Katie Shonk and Leah Kidwell provided editorial assistance.

turns to the salesperson, prepared to put his faith in the hands of someone who he thinks knows the answers to all of his questions.

Jack, the salesperson, explains that this dealership is different from all the others.

"I'm on your side," he says. "I'll do everything possible to get you a great deal."

Henry and Jack then spend the next hour and a half discussing various cars, test-driving one, and discussing the virtues of the dealership. Henry narrows his choices down to the car with a list price of $18,500 that he read about and test drove. He decides it's time for the bargaining to begin.

"Cars sure are expensive these days," Henry says, shaking his head. "I was hoping to find a nice one for about $14,000."

"I wish I could help you out, Hank, but those days are long gone," says Jack. "But I'm going to make sure you get a square deal. The question, is at what price can we realistically have you driving home today in your new car?"

"Well, this car doesn't have all the features I would like, but I'm willing to make some sacrifices if the price is right. Let's say, $16,000."

"Hank, no way can I go that low. The list price on this car is $18,500," says Jack. "I can get it for you for $18,000."

"That's too much," Henry says. "Listen, I know your invoice is about $16,000. I'll give you $16,200; that's $200 pure profit."

"My manager will never accept that. The dealership has overhead, advertising, and inventory costs to think about. They need to get a little cut of the action too. I may be able to get you the car for $17,500. Trust me, this is a very good price."

"I do trust you, Jack. However, I've checked out what this car is worth and I know what other people are paying for it. It's a nice car, but it's not the only one I'm considering. I'd be willing to pay $16,500 to eliminate the need to search more."

Jack tells Henry he'll have a talk with his sales manager. Twenty minutes later he returns.

"I really went to bat for you, Hank, because I respect you. And guess what? I have great news. My manager will let the car go for $17,000. I swear to you, I've never seen anyone get such a good deal in my 27 years in the business."

"What about my offer of $16,500?" Henry says.

"Boy, you just don't quit, do you Hank? But that's OK. You're a smart guy. Now listen, you know I would love to give you that price, but it's just impossible. Believe me."

"I do believe you. But I'm afraid I've wasted your time. I saw a car at another dealership that I like almost as much as this one, and I can get it for $16,000. Thanks, but no thanks." Henry turns to walk away.

"Wait a minute. Now hold on there a minute, Hank," says Jack. "You're a stubborn guy, aren't you? But I like that about you. Look, I want to sell you this car, even if it kills me. What do you say we split the difference 50–50? That's $16,750. You drive a hard bargain, but 50–50's fair, right?"

"Well, I guess it's fair. OK, you've got a deal."

Henry and Jack shake hands and fill out the initial paperwork. Then Jack leads Henry out of the showroom and into the business manager's office for the after-sale phase of the transaction. Here, Henry and the manager discuss the nuts and bolts of financing his new purchase. But while discussing expenses and the availability of loans for the car, the business manager also springs another option on Henry—the opportunity to purchase an extended warranty on his new acquisition.

Regaled with information on the bumper-to-bumper coverage this package provides, not to mention the peace of mind it ensures, Henry pays close attention to the business manager's pitch.

"This line of vehicle is built to last, of course, which is why you've decided to go with this car in the first place," the manager says. "But it's not a perfect world, and car malfunctions can be a part of life. And in the computer age, cars are more sophisticated and complex than ever before. Now, the engines in these cars are bulletproof; it's not going to break down if you provide the car with regular maintenance. But the electronics end—including the sunroof control computer, the temperature control module, the electronic fuel injection system, and the antilock braking system—they run into problems that can be very expensive."

While listening to the manager's tale of impending woe, Henry takes a mental inventory of the electronic components of his brand-new car. Is his purchase nothing more than a ticking time bomb?

"You know, something is probably going to happen to your car in the next six years," the manager continues. "That's why if you're buying this car and not leasing it, which is what you've decided to do, the coverage is worth it. It's factory-backed, and frankly, that's the only kind of coverage I would purchase if I was going to buy this car. Basically, you're taking the warranty that currently exists on the car and extending it, with the company backing up that promise. You get six years or 75,000 miles of parts and labor guaranteed, and from there it costs you nothing. The biggest thing these warranties do is freeze the cost of parts and labor. So, you pay for these things up-front now, and you won't have to pay any interest or rising prices for these items in the future."

"How often do these warranties pay out?" Henry asks.

"We pay claims on 70 percent of the warranties. So, if you go by the numbers, then there's a good chance—a 70 percent chance—that you're going to use it. It's worth it."

"How many of these claims actually recoup the amount of money sunk into the warranty?" Henry asks.

The business manager quickly changes the subject. Needless to say, Henry, who had been so buoyant only minutes ago about the prospect of driving off in his new car, is now in a bit of a panic. Is the service contract a good deal, or is it simply another way for the dealership to separate him and his bank account from even more funds? Henry decides to buy it, concerned that he could later regret passing on this option and facing a $1,500 repair.

As Henry pulls into his driveway, a neighbor stops by to admire the shiny new car.

"Did you get a good deal?" he asks.

"I got a great deal! I shaved $1,750 off the list price."

Wow, did Henry blow it! In this perfectly average trip to the car dealer, Henry made at least five money mistakes:

1. He created an environment in which the car dealership had the power.
2. He fell for the good guy, bad guy routine.

3. He accepted the 50–50 compromise because it sounded fair.

4. He bought the warranty.

5. Finally, Henry erroneously thinks he did well, thereby eliminating the possibility of learning from his failure.

Henry's trip was not a complete disaster since he kept open the option of going to a different dealership. Overall, however, he missed many important opportunities. The remainder of this chapter explores Henry's car-buying mistakes, and how they can be avoided in the future.

Who Has the Power?

Henry realized that the salesperson knew more than he did. As a result, Henry assumed that the dealership had the power. Before we let Henry go any further, let's decide if he is correct in feeling powerless. Consider the perspective of the dealership, and how thinking about the perspective of the dealer could have been helpful to Henry.

Recently, the Chevrolet Motor Division of General Motors ("Chevy") called me and asked me to teach my negotiations course to a group of owners of Chevy dealerships. I was delighted! As a negotiations professor, my classes always end up talking about buying houses and cars. As a consequence, I know lots of people who buy and sell houses and lots of people who buy cars. However, I usually only have the chance to talk to car dealers when I myself am buying a car. So I welcomed the chance to better understand the dealer's view of the negotiation process.

After the first morning of teaching, I had lunch with six of my students—all of them owners of Chevy dealerships. I pulled out the long list of questions I had written on the plane ride to Philadelphia and prepared to start my usual barrage (I do this often; it helps me learn as I go through life). Before I could open my mouth, the man to my left spoke up.

"Max, it's great that you're working with us today. We really need help with negotiations," Jim said.

"Yeah!" piped up Howard from across the table. "These customers are murder! It's not like it used to be."

"They have all the power," complained Lee. "These damn clipboards. I'm sick of them. It just isn't fair."

All around the table, everyone shook their heads in agreement. I must admit, I was caught off guard. "I'm confused," I said. "I often talk to people who are terrified of stepping foot in a car dealership. What do you mean, the customer has all the power? And what does a clipboard have to do with anything?"

"These clipboards find out our true dealer cost from the newspaper, *Consumer Reports*, and even worse, the Internet, where the data is updated and pretty accurate," Howard explained. "They walk in with their clipboards stuffed with data and offer us a tiny profit."

"They have too much information!" complained Lee.

I had caught on. A "clipboard" is a personality style of a well-informed customer, one not too popular with my lunchmates.

"How do the clipboards do?" I asked.

"We don't like them too much," grumbled Stacey.

"Yes, but what kind of deals do they get?" I asked.

"Well, if I realize that a clipboard isn't going to pay more than $200 over my real dealer cost, I'll take what he offers," said Rick. "If I don't, the next dealer five miles away will. Besides, I do get another chance to make money in the postsale—you know, financing, warranties, and insurance. If I don't make the sale, I don't get these other chances."

At this point, I was beginning to appreciate the owners' perspective; Henry did have the potential to have more power than the seller. Well-informed customers, or clipboards, are not popular, but they are effective. They know the other side's BATNA (Chapter 2), and they know their own—they can go to another dealer.

The plain truth is that there are simply more cars that Henry could buy than there are Henrys to buy them. Whichever car Henry wants, he has a number of places where he can make his purchase. That choice is power, and despite all the efforts of the salesperson to convince him otherwise, Henry, in fact, has more power than the dealer. Henry knows he wants to buy a small car, probably a two-door coupe, something reliable, with good gas mileage, and maybe a sunroof. Well, on that basis alone Henry has over 25 different models to choose from. What about car companies? Even if Henry is a highly decisive guy (he wants a two-door Honda Civic hatchback in racing red), a quick look in the yellow pages shows that from my home in Evanston (just north of Chicago), there are 11 different Honda dealerships close by.

So after shopping around and deciding what features are most important, Henry finds a car he likes. Great! Or Henry finds two or three cars that he has a difficult time deciding between. Even better! Remember, choice is power, and the more choices he has, the better deal he can get. If Henry decides that the only car for him is a 1999 convertible Ford Mustang in flame-fast fuchsia, he is limiting his bargaining power. If Henry would also consider buying a convertible Toyota Celica or Mitsubishi Eclipse, he would be better able to bargain down the salesperson. As with houses, never fall in love with just one car.

Well-informed customers can combine two critical ingredients for effectively negotiating with the car dealer: information and options. They can do homework to gather information such as the dealer's cost, and they can realize that they have options. In contrast, from the dealer's perspective, if the customer leaves, the dealership has lost a sale.

The Good Cop, Bad Cop Routine

Like most people, Henry was comforted by the friendly presentation of the salesperson, who explained that he was on Henry's side and that the sales manager was the problem. This is the standard good cop, bad cop routine. The basic structure is that the good cop (the customer's new friend, the salesperson) drags information out of you, the customer, and then blames any resistance from the dealership on the manager, the bad cop.

The good cop, bad cop routine works pretty well against naive negotiators. As a successful negotiator, however, always remember never to give any information or concession to the good cop that you would not want to give to the bad cop, for they are really on the same team. It is fine to be friendly with the good cop, but never yield any information or concession because of his or her pleasantness.

Many people are uncomfortable in the car dealership when the bad cop (the manager) emerges from the back room. They feel overwhelmed by the presence of an extra opponent. However, this is generally good news. When the salesperson is doing very well, the manager stays in the background. The manager's arrival implies that you are a viable customer, but not an easy one. In addition, the manager's presence allows you to negotiate directly with the decision maker, which you want to do. You can now convey your unwillingness to move beyond a certain level without first exercising your BATNA of comparison shopping.

50–50 Splits

At the end of Henry's bargaining session with the salesperson, he accepted the 50–50 proposal. After all, the salesperson met him halfway. Fifty-fifty is fair, isn't it? Maybe not. This 50–50 split, like many others, is really quite arbitrary. The final two numbers on the table were $16,500 and $17,000, the midpoint being $16,750. However, the first two numbers were the invoice price, $14,000, and the list price, $18,500, with a midpoint of $16,250. That's a $500 difference. Or look at it another way. Henry's first number was $14,000; the salesperson's was $18,000. Here we have a midpoint of $16,000, a difference of $750 from the agreed price. Which 50–50 offer is right? There is no right 50–50 split, simply lots of arbitrary numbers to split, and it is your job to make sure that you are splitting two numbers that work to your advantage.

A buyer should always keep in mind that a 50–50 split is a split *from* other numbers, and if the other numbers aren't fair, the 50–50 split will not be fair either. Whatever you can do to keep the initial offers low makes a 50–50 split more favorable to you. The successful negotiator realizes that there are multiple 50–50 splits available, is ready to propose the one that works to his or her advantage, and is ready to explain away an opponent's unfavorable 50–50 split.

Vivid Scares

Henry bought the extended warranty because he felt it would provide a measure of security and would be a good investment. Unfortunately, neither of Henry's assumptions was true. He fell victim to the salesperson's vivid scare.

Let's consider why so many car buyers fall for the pitch and purchase extended warranties. One reason may be that buyers believe that the extended warranty represents a good bargain. After all, even the most reliable cars need repairs, and you can probably recall garage bills that cost more than the warranty price. The typical $25 deductible seems like peanuts by comparison. Along with the aid of the salesperson's well-spun scenarios, you can easily imagine the financial hardship of enormous repair costs. When your point of reference is the thousands of dollars you just committed yourself to spending for the car, the money you put into the warranty appears minis-cule by comparison. As a result, you find yourself in a vulner-able position and naturally buy the extended warranty.

However, there are other issues to think about before buy-ing the contract. Almost all service contracts duplicate the man-ufacturer's warranty. That is, if your new car has a two-year, 24,000 mile warranty, and you buy the typical extended war-ranty of five years and 100,000 miles, what you are really pur-chasing is an additional three-year, 76,000 mile warranty. It's clearly in the dealer's interest to sell this to you. Based upon documents filed a few years ago in a lawsuit against Nissan, the typical extended warranty contract costing $795 was mostly pure profit for the dealer. Only $131 went to cover actual repairs; $109 went to Nissan for administrative costs, and the remaining $555 went to the dealer. In fact, according to the *New York Times*, many dealers get more of their profits from add-on products and services like this than from the actual sale of the car.[1] We will return to vivid scares and insurance in the next chapter.

Optimistic Illusions

Oddly enough, most people are satisfied with the outcome of their car purchase. Surveys also show that the vast majority of people think they *got a good deal* on their car. Part of a salesper-son's job is to convince you that you just made a great deal. In fact, try a quick survey with a group of your friends; virtually everyone will say they were pleased with the final result. The person who claims that he or she badly overpaid for a car is close to extinct. This is partially because people do not want to admit their mistakes to others, but even written or anonymous surveys show that, in fact, most people *do* think they got a good deal. Why?

Most people view themselves, the world, and the future in a considerably more positive light than is objectively likely. Individuals tend to perceive themselves as being better than others on a variety of desirable attributes,[2] causing them to have unrealistically positive self-evaluations.[3] For example, people perceive themselves as being better than others across such traits as honesty, cooperativeness, rationality, driving skill, negotiating skill, health, and intelligence.[4]

A common view among social psychologists is that positive illusions are adaptive.[5] These illusions are argued to contribute to psychological well-being by protecting an individual's positive sense of self and his or her motivation to persist at difficult tasks.[6] My view, shared by a growing number of scholars, is that positive illusions are likely to have a negative impact on learning and the quality of decision making. If you go through life confused by the belief that you are always doing well, you will never stop and ask how you can do better.

Preparation Advice for Henry— and for You

Do Your Homework

If you don't, you have relinquished your power, that is, information. Before you begin to negotiate the price of a car, know what you want. Do not test drive the car the day you are negotiating the price; figure out what you want first. This allows you to set the agenda and reduces the likelihood that your emotional desire to drive home in your car will affect your negotiation strategy. Besides, you know it will ride well—it's new! Learn about the car a month before it is time to buy. Figure out what you want, find out the dealer cost, identify your options, and then go negotiate.

Buying a car is generally the second most expensive purchase decision you will make, and, unlike many other decisions, you will probably do it several times during the course of your life. Many car buyers put themselves at a tremendous disadvantage by believing that the dealer and salesperson have more power than they do.

Set the Agenda with the Salesperson

If you do not set the agenda, the salesperson often will. The best example of this is price. For most car buyers, price is an important criterion—often the most important criterion—but never the only one. A buyer may also want to think about reliability, gas mileage, safety features, comfort, speed, and how well a particular car will retain its value. The salesperson, on the other hand, has only one item on his or her agenda: profit. The first significant words out of a salesperson's mouth are often, *"What monthly payment can you afford?"* Notice how this innocent, six-word question frames the decision process. It assumes all other options are secondary to price, it asks the *maximum* price you will pay (not what you want to pay), and sets a boundary of a *monthly*, not total, payment (since different financing options can achieve different total prices). If you tell salespeople what monthly payment you can afford, they will do their best to make you pay it. Once you have answered this question, you are playing the game on someone else's terms. As much as possible, figure out exactly what features you want, what order you want them in, and how much they are worth to you.

Realize the Power of Information

Probably nothing is changing the car buyer's access to information—and reducing the information advantage of the dealers—as much as the Internet. The Internet not only levels the information playing field, but it gives buyers even more choice than before, since one can shop on-line instead of having to go to a dealer's showroom. Although the number of car purchases made on-line is small, it is growing rapidly. Chrysler, which estimates that only 1.5 percent of its sales in 1996 were made on-line, believes that by the year 2000, 25 percent of its new car purchases will be made through the Internet.[7]

Aside from some advantages of purchasing on-line, which we will get to in a minute, the data available through the Internet helps reduce the disparity of information between you and the salesperson. In fact, often you can get more information than the salesperson, because you can find out about the cars at his dealership as well as those at other dealerships that interest you. And you don't even have to get on the highway. Services such as Microsoft CarPoint (www.carpoint.com), Edmund's Automobile Buyer's Guide (www.edmunds.com) and Intelli-Choice CarCenter (www.intellichoice.com) will give you the specifications of different models, product reviews, and advice from other buyers.

Does this mean, then, that you should be a clipboard? My recommendation is that you should prepare like a clipboard, but not show your clipboard (or detailed notes) to the salesperson. Be pleasant, but clear, in your unwillingness to pay above a certain level. Car dealers do not like clipboards, so don't annoy them. Instead, allow them to provide their best deal to a customer that they like. If safety is a primary concern, try the National Highway and Traffic Safety Administration (www.nhtsa.dot.gov) for a database of recalls, crash-test results, and consumer complaints. If you want help selecting a model that's based on your personal criteria, try DealerNet (www.dealernet.com) or AutoSite (www.autosite.com), which will match your choices to different models. Most of these services have many helpful features that are free, but if you are willing to shell out anywhere from $2 for information about a single car to about $10 for 30 days unlimited use, you can get access to a wealth of information. This includes information such as dealer invoice prices that enable you, just like the salesperson, to know how much money the dealer is making.

Understandably, once information is equal, the haggling is simplified and more in your favor. But if you just do not enjoy haggling, you can car shop on-line by simply listing the car (or cars) you are looking for and the features you want, include your telephone number, and wait for the phone to ring. The service company acts as a broker, relaying your information to dealers in your area and requiring them to quote you a price within a few days. The balance of power has shifted even more in the buyer's favor; instead of Henry driving from dealer to dealer to compare prices, he states his needs and dealers will bid for his business. For the dealers, this actually is not such a bad deal. They can cut their marketing costs from $400 or so per car to less than $50, and the quick sales let them turn over inventory faster.[8]

The biggest of the on-line broker services is Auto-By-Tel (www.autobytel.com) with over 1,600 dealers across America.[9] Other companies include AutoVantage (www.autovantage.com), AutobyInternet (www.autobyinternet.com), and Autoweb.com (www.autoweb.com). The influence of the Internet on dealerships is expected to mirror the explosion of other industries. Companies like Wal-Mart and Home Depot, for example, have used technological innovations and increased sales to crowd out smaller local merchandise or hardware stores, bringing lower prices to consumers. Once the buyer has the same information the seller does, it is a whole new game.

Finally, think through warranties and financing before you ever get to the dealer. Decision making under the influence of sales pressure is rarely wise. Remember, most of the after-sell items are pure profit to the dealer (more on this in Chapter 4).

Advice

Buying a car is easy because all the power belongs to the buyer. However, failing to follow some simple ideas gives power to the dealer and makes the purchase experience unpleasant. The next time that you buy a car:

- Be prepared. Walk into the dealership knowing what type of car you're considering, what type of features are important, and so forth.
- Recognize the power of being informed. Check out manufacturer prices, safety records, and other information on the Internet or in publications.
- Be aware that you have more options than the dealer. After all, you could shop elsewhere or choose a different make of car.
- Don't ever believe the salesperson is the good guy who is on your team rather than on the dealer's team.
- Remember that 50–50 is not necessarily fair.
- Don't buy the warranty.

4

VIVID SCARES

*L*ast year, I broke my standard "no warranties" rule. My spouse, Marla, needed a new computer. For her birthday, I decided to buy her one and to have it professionally installed. So, with the help of Jim, our trusted computer advisor, I selected a $1,600 computer at Best Buy in Evanston. The salesperson offered me the opportunity to buy a dealer's warranty—$100 for four years. While I realized immediately that this wasn't a good value (more on this later in the chapter), I thought that $100 was a small price to pay to avoid being criticized by my spouse when the computer broke down.

Two months later, the mouse stopped working. Here is an opportunity to collect on the warranty, I thought, so I headed off to the store with the broken mouse. At customer service, I was told that they would happily send the mouse back to Compaq, and get it back to me within the month. When I insisted that I needed a mouse now to operate the computer, they offered to sell me one. "No! That's why I bought the warranty!" I complained. But they insisted that the delay wasn't covered by the warranty. After much arguing back and forth, they realized that I wasn't going to go away easily. They loaned me a used mouse, and promised to call within the month when the new mouse arrived.

Amy Binder provided research and writing assistance on this chapter, and Katie Shonk and Leah Kidwell provided editorial assistance.

Surprise, surprise—they never called back, and we forgot all about the broken mouse. After all, our loaner was working fine. But after two months had passed, the loaner mouse suddenly stopped working. Off to Best Buy again, where I was told that I must be mistaken. They had no record of my previous visit, and they do not lend out mice. "Can I see the manager?" I asked. "Sorry, but this is Sunday," they said. They managed to get rid of me by giving me a $10 mouse, and I brought it home so that Marla could get back to her fiction writing.

My multiple visits to Best Buy, the broken commitments of the dealer, and the sheer annoyance caused by an inexpensive piece of plastic made the warranty far less valuable than was suggested by the presentation of the salesperson. Keeping my $100 and simply buying a new mouse would have been a far better and simpler strategy.

You have probably been in similar situations. At one time or another, we have all faced the anxiety-provoking decision of whether it is wiser to pay additional fees to protect ourselves from future ill fortune or to turn our backs on the sales pitch. It turns out that we say yes far too often.

As we saw in the last chapter, purchasing large-ticket items such as a car can be fraught with peril unless you arm yourself with information before going in to deal and also have several options to give you bargaining power. But there are some aspects of making an expensive purchase that may be more difficult for the customer to anticipate. Remember the tough decision Henry had to make when the dealer recommended an extended warranty, a purchase intended to give him peace of mind? Or how the business manager played on Henry's fears of electronic malfunction, and quoted a 70 percent payment on claims? It is often difficult for consumers to turn their backs on such offers because the sales pitch has prodded them to imagine their worst fears. Salespeople are practiced at the art of such vivid scares.

Now, take a few minutes to solve the following two problems:

1. Add up all the money you have paid for optional insurance in the last two years. Include all warranties, car rental insurance, and so forth.
2. Add up the amount of insurance you have collected on those insurance policies and warranties.

Most people can remember those occasions when they were glad that they were covered by insurance or a warranty. For the vast majority of people, however, simply putting the money spent on optional coverage in a separate account would leave plenty of funds to pay for the occasional repair and would probably leave enough for a nice vacation. This rule of thumb holds true despite the fact that most people tend to forget the number of excess warranties they have purchased.

Whether at the new car dealer where we are offered an extended warranty, at the rental car counter where we are advised to purchase collision, theft, and liability insurance, or at the cash register contemplating the additional warranty on our new stereo or computer, we are frequently faced with pressures from agents to buy more optional coverage than we may actually need. Sometimes we resist this pressure and other times we do not. What makes us vulnerable to hard sells, even if we have the lurking suspicion that they are a waste of money?

Let's look at another example. Arriving in Boston on a business trip, Leah goes to the Zippee Rent-A-Car counter to pick up the automobile she has reserved. The agent asks her if she would like to purchase insurance for the duration of her rental, and when she declines, he uses scare tactics to pressure Leah into changing her mind. "Do you have any insurance?" he asks. "Are you aware of the company's policy on repairing damaged cars?" "Are you sure you're covered in the case of bodily injury?"[1]

In similar situations, many of us succumb to the siren song of sure insurance coverage, even if we suspect that we are already covered by either our own automobile insurance policy or by the credit card we are using to rent the car. The purchase of unneeded or unwanted insurance at car-rental counters across the country adds up to an estimated $1.2 billion per year in profit for the car–rental companies.

There are many opportunities floating around the marketplace on which you can spend your hard-earned cash. Approximately 30 percent of new car buyers purchase extended warranties (also known as service contracts), totaling $4 billion a year.[2] And when it comes to smaller-ticket items, such as VCRs, stereos, and refrigerators, the proportion of extended warranties bought per purchase is even higher. According to *Consumer Reports*, about 40 percent of the people who shop at electronics and appliance stores purchase them.[3] Are you among this 40 percent?

The trade-off being made in these transactions is your money for some peace of mind. Following are some of the most common policies that are offered to ease your anxiety—policies against which financial planners routinely counsel:[4]

- *Credit card insurance.* These policies promise to protect your credit cards against losses incurred if the cards are stolen or unlawfully used. But most credit cards limit your liability if you quickly notify the company that the card is missing.

- *Credit life/credit disability policies.* These pay off the balance on a loan if you die, and pay off parts of an outstanding loan if you are incapacitated. According to a *Money* magazine article, the majority of the 20 million or so Americans who spend $2 billion on credit life insurance get a terrible deal. This is because credit life insurance frequently costs three times as much as basic term life insurance, with premiums averaging $7 for each

$1,000 in coverage versus less than $2 per every $1,000 for a typical term policy for a nonsmoking middle-aged man. However, credit life insurance is a cash cow for the banks that sell it; commissions average 40 percent of premiums versus approximately 5 percent for mutual funds and annuities. Not surprisingly, then, many banks are apt to push it aggressively, regardless of its debatable worth to customers.[5]

- *Hospital indemnity insurance.* These policies typically promise daily payments of between $75 and $100 for a hospital stay. But even one day in a hospital can cost thousands of dollars—insurance payoffs are usually just a drop in the bucket.

Title Insurance

Title insurance is another type of policy that customers frequently purchase to ease their minds while buying a home. Think back to when you were closing on your last house. Do you remember the seemingly endless number of checks you were required to write at that time: one for the mortgage, one for the lawyer's fees, one for documentation fees, one for an escrow account, and one for title insurance, among others? While all of the items on this list are financially burdensome to the signer, the purpose of most of them is pretty clear in the purchaser's mind. But title insurance has the unique feature of being both expensive and misunderstood. Did you know what you were buying when you shelled out the approximately $1,000 you paid for it?

Sold exclusively when you close on a new house, title insurance promises to pay for the legal defense of your property in the event that a claim is made against your home after it has been transferred to your name. If the defense is unsuccessful, the title company will pay the expenses that you incur, as well as the expenses your lending institution incurs, assuming you have a mortgage. Title insurance companies advertise that they cover such risks as incorrect information on deeds and mortgages and incorrect references in public records; that they protect against liens, which are claims against the property that might survive transfer of the property (for example, unpaid taxes, mortgages, and sewer and water assessments); that they cover other claims of ownership, such as a spouse or child who was not mentioned in a former owner's will; and that they protect against invalid deeds, which are transfers by previous sellers who lacked the authority to sell, such as minors or the mentally incompetent. What title insurance does *not* cover, however (unless a formal geographical survey has been made), are property boundary disputes—such as fencing in the wrong location.[6] While property disputes are perhaps the most common legal claim made against home owners, they are one of the standard exclusions found in many title insurance policies.

While we may not know a single home owner who has ever made use of his or her title insurance policy (and most home owners do own one of these policies), the sales agents for these companies have an extensive repertoire to convince us their policies are necessary. There we are, buying a home, making one of the biggest investments we will probably ever make, and the hazards of our decision loom large. Read the following on-line sales pitch that one title insurance company used to attract its potential customers, and imagine hearing similar arguments at the time of closing on a new property:

> Buying a home is often the biggest investment consumers make in a lifetime. Transferring clear title to that home is a complicated task with many pitfalls. Because land typically has many owners with many different rights that have attached to it over time, it is important to insure that title is transferred accurately and free and clear of other's

rights. You can protect your investment by acquiring *Own-ers Title Insurance* [emphasis added].

Unlike a car, land is permanent and has the poten-tial for many different types of unforeseen title defects. Even though title companies engage in a thorough title search to verify the Seller's right to transfer ownership and even though they search to discover liens, unpaid taxes, restrictions limiting the use of the property, unsat-isfied mortgages or judgments, etc. . . , sometimes searches are flawed and there are many title defects that even a thorough search won't uncover.[7]

Also choosing to emphasize the uncertainty that accrues to property that has changed hands many times over the years, another company writes on its web page, "Even if you are buying a new home, the property has existed for millions of years. Predecessors to the current recording and ownership tracking systems have been in place for the last four-hundred years."[8]

Heady warnings, indeed. One is left to wonder if Nean-derthal-drafted property laws supersede modern legal regula-tions, or if the great-great-great-great-great grandson of the first owner of the house is just around the corner waiting to nail you for his rightful property! In any case, a title insurance policy, at about $500 to $1,500 on most homes (premiums vary from state to state), can reduce your anxiety, allowing you to sleep better under your new roof. As such, many experts offer the following kind of advice to protect you from worst-case scenarios:

In general, title insurance has proven itself to be a wise purchase for most homebuyers. It dramatically reduces the possibility that you will be drawn into a long drawn-out legal battle when some ex-wife of a long-ago owner shows up and claims her ex-husband forged her name to the deed when he sold the house as part of their divorce settlement. For most homebuyers, it is a mistake not to buy title insurance.[9]

I disagree! The problem is that you are spending money that has only the remotest likelihood of being used in your interest and that instead goes a long way toward filling the coffers of the insurance company. According to *Barron's*, title insurance companies are the envy of their insurance industry colleagues because their loss ratios are currently running at about 6–7 percent of their revenues.[10] This means that for every $100 you and others spend on the insurance policies, the insurance companies are only paying out $6–$7 on claims. That's a huge profit margin built on the backs of anxious home owners. While these numbers may make title insurance executives and investors happy, they certainly do not paint the rosiest picture for the customer.

Unfortunately, even if home buyers do wise up to the bad deals these policies seem to offer, there may not be much they can do about it, unless they are able to pay for their homes without the assistance of a mortgage. Since most mortgage-lending institutions require borrowers to purchase enough insurance to cover their loans, customers are increasingly held captive to title insurance. Short of an insurrection against bank requirements, buyers may be stuck with an additional $1,000 worth of fees at closing. However, buyers may have one small trick available to them. There are two types of coverage offered by title insurance companies—lender's policies and owner's policies—and often only the owner's coverage comes with an additional premium.[11] New home owners may be able to save a few hundred dollars by purchasing a lender's insurance policy, which pays off the balance on a mortgage loan, rather than an owner's policy, which pays off the balance on a mortgage loan in addition to compensating home owners for the value of the homeowner's equity.

Even if we are stuck with this form of coverage, the issue

of title insurance brings up three important questions. First of all, why do banks require that buyers purchase policies they rarely need? Secondly, why do people at the closing on their home unquestioningly submit to buying title insurance when they have only a vague understanding of what it is covering? Thirdly, why do people who don't have mortgages (and don't have to follow a lender's rules) still purchase title insurance? The answer to these questions also explains why we buy extended warranties on our new cars, rental car insurance, and hospital insurance. We will explain the psychology behind these purchases later in the chapter.

Sounds Good, but Where's the Payoff?

Watchdogs of warranties say that products—from small- to big-ticket items—last longer today than they did years ago. According to *Consumer Reports,* less than 10 percent of extended warranties for appliances and electronics are ever used, and they tend instead to be big moneymakers for their sellers.[12] As part of a series on extended warranties, the magazine counseled readers that the plans waste their money. "Buying an extended warranty is a risky proposition," *Consumer Reports* stated. "It's like making two bets: that the appliance will break down after the manufacturer's warranty expires . . . and that the cost of the repairs will exceed the cost of the contract. In our view, that's a long shot."[13]

As if this news were not bad enough, sometimes the rules the store has laid out are not even honored.[14] I thought that I had a simple agreement with Best Buy, but I did not. Fixing my mouse turned out to be a very complicated process. Sometimes, the lack of follow-through is more extensive, such as when a retailer goes out of business, leaving customers with worthless warranties. It's important that consumers know who is backing the warranties they purchase.

In some situations, car manufacturers sell the contracts to their dealers, who then sell them to their customers. These arrangements are usually pretty secure, since the manufacturer is likely to still be in business to deliver the warranted work. But in other cases, the dealers may sell extended warranties that are backed by financial-service or insurance companies. These warranties become worthless if the backer goes out of business. Much to their consternation, customers have found that the bankrupt issuers then fail to honor contracts, or that their telephone lines are constantly busy, causing customers no small amount of frustration as they try to make good on their deal.[15] Unfortunately, such situations are not so rare. Of the one hundred or so independent underwriters that operate across the country, fifteen of them have gone out of business in the past three years, according to reports by the National Automobile Dealers Association.[16]

Vivid Makes Livid

So, back to the question of why so many of us purchase these policies and contracts. Do you notice any similarities in the pitches our friendly sales representatives make in the preceding examples? All of them are relying on vivid scares to lure the customer into a deal. As we discussed earlier, vivid events make a great impression on our imaginations, and stories about electronic component failure, liability suits, and expensive medical treatment and hospital stays leave us susceptible to pitches such as those delivered by the rental car agent and the salesclerk. After all, everyone wants to avoid future repair costs on a new car or big-screen TV. Who would not want to protect themselves against huge losses from liability in the event of an accident in a rental car? What parent does not cringe at the thought of burdening their dependents upon death with their credit card debt (in the case of credit life insurance)? And it seems reasonable to take measures that will shield us from overwhelming hospital fees (in the case of hospital indemnity insurance).

The answer to the question of why we buy coverage even when it is a bad idea has to do with the vividness of the information with which we are presented. When we are at the car lot listening to the salesclerk's cautionary tales, we take in the information selectively, even if that selection is unconscious. Whenever we evaluate a purchase option, we pay attention to certain facts about the future and ignore others. The facts to which we are most likely to pay attention (and to which our attention is often *drawn* by the selling agents) present us with vivid reminders of the consequences of *not* buying the additional coverage, be it insurance or extended warranty. We may pay attention to these facts even when they are mostly irrelevant to the final outcome.

All of us have had either personal experience with the kinds of negative situations the sales clerk is describing, or we have heard stories about such frightening scenarios from other sources. Whether we have heard these accounts from our friends, in the media, or through the grapevine ("I heard Tom was in an accident, and boy did he have to pay big . . ."), the intensity of some case of bad fortune causes us to imagine our own possible future outlay of cash. The possibility of such costs, backed by the images that are conjured up in these stories, leads us to make bad decisions at the point of purchase.

What is it about the vividness of these stories that causes us to be vulnerable to sales agents' pitches? Researchers have found that one shining example of an event can have a far greater effect on people's attitudes and behavior than mountains of proven, but mundane, data. An example of the effects of vividness can be seen in the huge spike in insurance policy purchases for earthquake protection in the Midwest. How did salespeople draw on policyholders' dread of losing everything in the "Big One?" A climatologist and business consultant from New Mexico named Iben Browning made news when he predicted that there was a 50 percent chance that an earthquake with a magnitude of 6.5 to 7.5 on the Richter scale would occur along the New Madrid fault on December 3, 1990. While anyone can predict an earthquake and not receive press coverage, the media were highly responsive to Browning and his forecast. He made his projection during television "sweeps" week, when shows are competing most heavily for viewers.

Even though expert geologists generally dismissed Browning's prognostication, insurance companies began recording a blitz in earthquake insurance coverage. Allstate and State Farm saw applications for earthquake insurance skyrocket. Spotting the trend, several insurance agencies quickly jumped on the bandwagon and began sending out mass mailings featuring the December 3 prediction. Berent and Co., an insurance firm based in Skokie, Illinois, issued a newsletter to 900 of its policyholders that bore the headline, "Prepare Your Home To Ride Out Some Quake Damage." Not surprisingly, December 3, 1990, produced no such earthquake. As suggested in this chapter, it is the vividness and saliency of the earthquake prediction that prompted many thousands of people to overestimate the probability of its occurrence.

In addition to being affected by the vividness of scares like this, our behavior is also shaped by the frequency and timing with which we experience events. In other words, we are more likely to recall an event if it has happened numerous times and if it has happened recently. Many managers conducting performance reviews, for example, work from memory (which, as we know, is subject to bias). The vivid instances relating to an employee that are more easily recalled from memory (both favorable and unfavorable) will appear to be more numerous and will therefore be weighted more heavily in performance appraisal. Managers also give more weight to performance during the three months prior to the evaluation than to the previous nine months of the evaluation period.

The same thing is said to happen with judging nominations for the Academy Awards. It is folk wisdom that films released in the latter part of the year have a greater chance of being recalled by the voters and selected as Best Picture. Because memories of these films are fresher in the minds of the voters, this bias favors the late entries.

Yet another example of the power of the *recency effect* is witnessed every day on television. Many consumers are annoyed by repeated exposure to the same advertising message and wonder why the advertiser does not give more useful information, rather than repeating the same information again and again. After all, we are smart enough to understand it the first time! Unfortunately, both the frequency and the vividness of the message have been shown to affect our purchasing behavior. Bombardment of repeated, uninformative messages makes the product more easily recalled from memory and is often the best way to get us to buy a product.[17]

Another pair of researchers have suggested that because of our susceptibility to vividness and recency—as demonstrated in the examples above—we become particularly prone to overestimating unlikely events.[18] For instance, if we actually witness a house burning down as opposed to just reading about it in the newspaper, we are much more prone to think that house fires happen fairly often. The direct observation of an event makes it much more salient to us.

It is little wonder then that we respond with our wallets to the vivid scares produced for us by insurance agents, salespeople, and car dealers when they ask us whether we want to protect ourselves from the future costs of injury or repair. We are all certainly well aware of the high costs associated with illness and faulty merchandise, and the pictures these sales agents paint for us tap into our knowledge of the possibility of these events, even if the possibility is remote. We are not being irrational when we respond to these manufactured scares; rather, the agents are successfully manipulating our decision biases.

When and How to Buy Insurance

Yes, there are times to buy insurance. You should insure yourself against realistic risks that have reasonable possibilities, when you cannot afford the loss. You should also insure the future of people you care about through life insurance, for example. But as we have discussed, you should pass on the endless opportunities to be a victim of a vivid scare. You should also pass on insuring losses that are affordable. If you simply pass on insuring the affordable losses, you will have lots of extra money that can be used to pay for the occasional loss, and you will be able to buy other goods with the extra money you have saved. Thus, there are times to buy insurance, but fewer times than intuition would suggest.

Once you do decide to buy insurance, one cost-saving technique is to raise your deductibles to reduce your premiums. There's no need to insure for the amount that you can afford to lose. If someone is selling you insurance, it is because they have determined that it is a profitable opportunity for them—not for you!

Another strategy is to come armed with both the knowledge about our susceptibility to vivid stories (such as those presented to us by appliance sales clerks) and savvy about the bad deals that these pitches represent. When we come fully loaded with these two forms of information, we will be able to stare down the frightening images of bankruptcy, home eviction, natural disaster, and personal injury that salespeople let loose on our imaginations and, at the same time, hold on tight to our wallets.

Finally, make your insurance and warranty decisions before buying the commodity. Never buy impulsive, uninformed vivid scare insurance under the influence of a salesperson who makes money if you say yes. Then, once you start passing on insurance, put the savings in a separate investment account. When you finally lose money on a specific loss based on the advice in this chapter, simply pay the loss from all of the money you have saved over the years by not buying unnecessary insurance.

Advice

The first step in determining whether to buy insurance is to be well educated. Ask the following questions about the insurance type and do your homework:

- How often do people gain by buying this insurance?
- How much money are the insurance company and the intermediaries who sell the insurance making?
- Are you already covered for the loss through other insurance?
- Can you afford to incur the loss?

If the answer to any of these questions discourages you from buying the insurance, it rarely makes sense to spend the money.

Chapter

5

TIME'S UP: HOW MUCH IS YOUR TIME WORTH?

*W*hen I first started studying judgment and decision making, I was fascinated by the biases that my colleagues and I were discovering. I assumed that once I identified these biases, and thought up methods for correcting them, I myself would become immune to them. In fact, I became hyperaware of my responsibility, as an observer of the flaws and foibles of the average Joe, to hold myself up as an exemplary model of rational thought and action. As a professor teaching negotiation, I had an obligation to get a good deal on all my major purchases. My students were constantly asking, "What did you pay?"

It was in this spirit of attempting to behave by the book—books and articles written by me and my friends—that I approached the purchase of a big-screen TV. I did exactly what I thought I should do. I spent a great deal of time learning about various manufacturers and models. I checked out articles that told me about the cost of TVs to dealers. I found multiple dealers that had the TV that I was interested in buying and visited each a number of times. In the final negotiation, I bundled the price with a VCR, a satellite dish, and

---

Amy Binder and Katie Shonk provided writing and editorial assistance on this chapter. Leah Kidwell provided a final edit.

in-house installation, which is very important to me since I have lit-tle technical skill. I obtained one last price concession by mention-ing that I had a good alternative—a competitor's store.

I came home quite proud of my purchase. "How did you do?" asked Marla, my spouse. I proudly related the story of my success to her. Marla listened patiently and then asked, "So, in the last 20 hours of your search, how much extra money did you save?" I thought about her question, and proudly announced that I saved about $120. Marla smiled. "Max, are you looking for extra work for $6 an hour?" she asked.

I made a number of mistakes during my search for the perfect deal on a TV, but the biggest one was ignoring the value of my precious (at least in my own mind) time.

Thousands of experts get rich giving workshops and lectures on the best way to organize and delegate our time at work, and numerous businesses cater to busy professionals who need help managing their time. Professionals are looking for ways to squeeze more quality time out of their day—time for their spouses, their children, hobbies, entertainment, and sports. The so-called experts, however, typically offer stopgap advice and services. Buy an expensive daily planner, they advise, hire a company to shop for your groceries, make to-do lists and flow charts until you turn blue in the face. These temporary cures are often not worth the big-ticket price because this advice fails to get at the heart of the matter—the mistakes we make with our time and the reasons we make these mistakes.

While most professionals consider time to be their most valuable resource, they often squander it in their attempts to conserve another important resource: money. As we learn in this chapter, our failure to budget time wisely, and therefore to budget money wisely, arises from cognitive mistakes of which most people are unaware. As my experience buying a TV shows, even a self-proclaimed expert on decision making is not im-mune to the biases that are hard-wired into our brains.

In this chapter, I discuss a variety of timing biases that affect the way we spend our time and our money. One useful question to ask as you get started is "How much is an hour of my time worth?" My guess is that you too often give up an hour for far less than this amount. The goal of this chapter is to provide you with an opportunity to think about how you actually trade off your time and money in comparison with how you would prefer to trade off your time and money.

What's Your Time Worth?

Read the following quiz item:[1]

Imagine that you are about to purchase a calculator for $50. The salesperson informs you that the calculator you wish to buy is on sale at the other branch of the store, which is a 20 minute drive from where you are now. What is the highest price that you would be willing to pay for the calculator at the other store such that you would be willing to travel there for the discount?

Jot down your answer and then consider the next question:[2]

Imagine that you are about to purchase a color television for $500. The salesperson informs you that this television is on sale at the other branch of the store, which is a 20 minute drive from where you are now. What is the highest price that you would be willing to pay for the TV at the other store such that you would be willing to travel there for the discount?

A rational analysis would suggest that you should have required the same discount in each problem. In both cases, the costs would be 20 minutes of your time, plus gas, parking, and so forth. For the trip to be worthwhile, the benefits (money saved) should exceed the value you place on the costs. Since the costs are the same in both cases, the minimum discount required should be the same in both cases.

However, chances are you didn't answer the two questions with the same dollar discount required to make the trip. Rather, your answer depended on the price of the item you were buying, or, more specifically, on the supposed bargain you thought that you were getting. Specifically, you required a greater discount in absolute dollars to travel to buy the television than to buy the calculator. A promised savings of $25 on the $50 calculator (a 50 percent discount) may entice you to make the drive, whereas saving $25 on the $500 TV (a 5 percent discount) does not seem worth the trip.

This discrepancy just doesn't make sense. Spending twenty minutes in the car to save $25 for a calculator but refusing to drive as far to save an equal amount on a television is a money mistake. We should be able to come up with a constant dollar figure that will determine whether or not we will go out of our way for a bargain, no matter what we are buying, or what percentage of discount we are getting. Why do we fail to behave rationally in this situation?

Our purchases are affected by the value we place on a commodity—in this case, how much the TV or calculator is worth to us—and by the quality of the deal that we get. Value describes the usefulness or satisfaction we get from a purchase in comparison to what we paid for it. Imagine that you visited a vineyard in France on your honeymoon and sampled its wine. Since the trip, you and your spouse have bought a bottle of the expensive wine on special occasions. The wine has high value for you and your spouse; you don't mind paying the high price because it has great sentimental value to you.

We also care a great amount about the quality of the deal we receive on a particular item, which is determined by what we believe the item should cost. One measure of a deal's quality might be how good the story will sound when you tell your friends about your great bargain. Most people, when confronting the TV and calculator question, give too much weight to the deal quality of the purchase. Rather than being dazzled by irresistible sales—50, 60, 70 percent off!—you should keep in mind the amount of money you are spending and the amount you are actually saving.

I have taught many classes on negotiation in Thailand, and have found that the task of negotiating for a taxi in Bangkok illustrates the tendency to overweight the quality of a deal. In Bangkok, before you get into the taxi, you negotiate the price of the trip. If you do not speak Thai, you hold up fingers (1 finger = 10 Baht = 40 cents [U.S.], 2 fingers = 20 Baht = 80 cents, 3 fingers = 30 Baht = $1.20, etc.). No trip within Bangkok costs more than 70 Baht ($2.80). Each day in class, my students would ask where I went the previous night, and how much I paid the taxi driver to get home. They would then evaluate my performance. I thought that I had gotten very good at this game, at least until Marla arrived. One night, we were returning home from across town, and I had two negotiations in a row in which I offered 30 Baht ($1.20), while the taxi driver countered at 40 Baht ($1.60). As a result, we reached an impasse. Ten minutes later, I paid 30 Baht, but at the added expense of some needling from Marla once again on the value of my (not to mention her) time. Of course, this example is a little different from the TV purchase, since the quality of the deal was important for the next day's class—or at least I can use my class as a justification.

One more personal experience demonstrates how the power of the quality of the deal influences even a supposed expert. When I was growing up, my family always clipped coupons—this was a major activity on Sunday mornings when the big newspaper arrived. At the age of four, I clipped coupons because my parents told me to. By the age of eight, I knew that we were doing this to save money. The more interesting question is, why was I still clipping coupons at the age of thirty? After thinking hard about these kinds of problems, I assessed what I was getting paid for my weekly chore. It added up to about $6 an hour for less than an hour per week. My current strategy is to dump the advertising section in the recycling container without even taking a look!

A caveat: some students who have heard me lecture on this topic have argued that the discussion is too money focused. They argue that if you take this argument far enough, well-paid professionals would never cook or garden, since they do not save much money doing these tasks. These students argue that they get great enjoyment from growing food and preparing it themselves, and reject the notion that these behaviors are irrational. I agree with them. If you find the task enjoyable, then by all means do it! However, I personally find no enjoyment in clipping coupons, running around to every appliance store in town, or standing on a corner in Bangkok on a very muggy night trying to save 40 cents.

Managing Deadlines

When I teach negotiations, I almost always set up one-on-one role plays. Most of the time, I provide the students with a time constraint, such as, "You have 90 minutes to conduct the negotiation." After the negotiations, I put the results of all the dyads on the board and find out from the students what worked and what did not. I will usually point out a pair in which the buyer got a great deal at the expense of the seller. When I ask the seller why they caved in so much, a common response is, "I ran out of time." I then ask that seller, "What about the buyer, didn't he or she run out of time as well?" For the first time, the seller realizes that the deadline affected them both.

Time management is a particularly critical factor in negotiation. We all know that a great deal happens as the deadline approaches. How does time affect who wins? First of all, both sides lose by negotiating under pressure; parties are far less likely to find mutually beneficial trades. But looking strictly at the distributive aspect of negotiation, the party who is more patient gets more of the pie. The party who is obsessed with meeting the deadline feels a greater need to make a concession in order to get the deal done. Expert salespeople use this weakness to their advantage; they patiently wait for you to become impatient and wrap up the deal.

At most bookstores in the United States, if you go to the business section, you can find books on how to negotiate with the Japanese, the Chinese, Europeans, and so forth. These books tend to offer overly simplistic advice that stereotypes entire cultures. While you should always be prepared when traveling to another country, you should avoid accepting these gross stereotypes. This should be obvious when we turn the tables. When I travel overseas, I often visit bookstores and find plenty of advice on how to negotiate with Americans. The essence of this advice comes back to patience. These books will tell you that Americans are an impatient group; they need to get the deal done now. So, the logic goes, the best way to negotiate against them is to get nothing done early in the negotiation, and as the deadline approaches (such as their flight back to the United States), Americans will start making concessions to close the deal.

Obviously, not all Americans are impatient. This advice doubtless leads to highly inefficient negotiations when stalling tactics backfire. Nevertheless, this advice is useful in highlighting the significant role of patience in negotiations.

How do you manage impatience? First, assess whether you really *do* need the deal done now, or whether this is simply a psychological preference arising from boredom, frustration, and so forth. If it is only a psychological preference, recognizing your weakness will help you strengthen your resolve and control your impatience. Being patient in negotiation is a developed skill that can be used to your strategic advantage.

On the other hand, your own impatience can be a useful signal that the negotiation you are engaged in is a waste of your time. I am always annoyed by the prospect of hanging out at a car dealership. Car salespeople often work under the assumption that the more time you spend with them, the greater the likelihood that you will buy a car. To counter this belief, I often let the salesperson know, very early, that I am willing to buy a car that day, but that I only have 40 minutes available. I also convey comfort with the idea of walking away with no car, leaving it unclear whether my next visit would be to that dealership or to one of its competitors. Now, time is on my side. The dealership needs to quickly make concessions in order to keep me from leaving the showroom without a car.

Intertemporal Choices: Save It for Later

Would you rather have one free dinner now or three free dinners five years from now? Would you be willing to pay $100 to save $18 each year for the next ten years? Would you vote to pay 50 cents more per gallon of gas in order to reduce the federal deficit, thus benefiting future generations but not yourself?

We often face questions such as these concerning the degree to which we discount the future. Intertemporal decisions involve the biggest issues in our lives, ones that strongly affect our finances: when to get married, when to buy a house, when to have children, when to begin saving for retirement. Therefore, it's important that we become aware of the mistakes that result from timing effects.

The "I want it now" phenomenon is a common intertemporal bias that infiltrates immediate monetary decisions as well as ones that we make over time. Think of the times you have bought something on impulse, only to regret the purchase at the end of the month when you got your credit card bill. Suddenly that rowing machine gathering dust in a corner of your bedroom doesn't look so dazzling when you realize you'll be paying it off for months to come. We explore the complexities of internal money conflicts—"want" versus "should"—more thoroughly in Chapter 8.

Discounting the future also leads to unwise spending and investment patterns. Research shows the use of extremely high discount rates with regard to the future.[3] Most home owners do not have enough insulation in their attics and walls and do not buy more expensive, energy-efficient appliances even when they would recoup the extra costs in less than a year. A simple way to save money is to conduct an energy audit on your house. Many utility companies provide this service for a small fee. When you get their report, implement the good ideas that you receive! Most of us are currently passing on significant money saving opportunities all around our house.

Beyond being short-sighted, discounting of the future may be selfish from an intergenerational, global, and environmental perspective.[4] That is, when we contribute to the national deficit or chop down the rain forest, our generation benefits at the expense of future generations. Interestingly, most people agree that we should leave the earth in at least as good a condition as we found it, or that we should not treat the earth "as if it were a business in liquidation."[5] However, because we often give insufficient attention to problems that are in the distance, our ongoing decisions are inconsistent with our attitudes.[6] As a result, we make decisions that are against our long-term best interests, and often injure other parties.

Advice

Time is critical in many of our decisions, and the misuse of time leads to numerous money mistakes. This chapter highlights three areas in which time matters:

1. *The value that you place on your time.* Be aware: Think about the value of your time and how to manage it better. What annoying tasks are you currently doing that can be eliminated or transferred to others who are more interested in doing them, creating a better life for yourself?

2. *How you manage time under the threat of a deadline.* Recognizing that you will need to adjust how you manage time, rearrange your schedule. Think through strategies before the deadline approaches.

3. *How you make trade-offs across time.* Make changes in your purchasing decisions to maximize long-term benefits. Before you buy a new couch, ask where it will be in five years. If the answer isn't your living room, maybe you should reconsider the purchase.

As with the other mistakes described in this book, there is no reason for you to believe that you are immune from any of these biases. Take it from an expert who has fallen into these traps time and time again! Now, when it is time to buy a new TV, I do get a very good price. However, I am willing to sacrifice a final $50 or so in savings if I can save five hours in the process. By conscientiously looking for timing errors in your behavior, you will become adept at eliminating them from your repertoire.

6

HAVE I GOT A MUTUAL FUND FOR YOU!

*M*y friend Ryan received a free copy of an investor newsletter that advised him that it was a good time to sell stock because, its experts predicted, the market would fall in the next six months. Ryan ignored the newsletter, but later learned that its prediction had been correct: The market fell dramatically. Six months later, Ryan received another free copy of this newsletter. This time, the experts predicted that the market would rise over the next six months. Ryan showed the newsletter to me and told me about the accuracy of its previous prediction. He said that although he had been stung by the market in recent years, he was impressed by the newsletter's last prediction and was thinking about following its most recent advice. However, when I strongly advised Ryan not to let the newsletter influence his investment decisions, he decided to follow his gut instinct and hold off on buying new stock.

When six months had once again passed, Ryan received a third free copy of the newsletter. Once again, the newsletter pointed

Leah Kidwell provided research and draft writing for a part of this chapter and did a final edit. Writing and editing assistance was provided by Katie Shonk.

out the success of its predictions, and again the editors advised their readers to continue buying stocks for the next six months.

"Max, they've made consistently accurate predictions over the past year!" Ryan said to me. "I don't know how they do it, but I'm beginning to feel that I can trust their advice."

"Well, I don't want to tell you how to spend your money, Ryan, but just last week you complained to me that you don't have as much disposable income as you'd like."

"That's true, but when I think of the money I might have had today if I had followed the newsletter's advice in the first place . . ."

Ryan ended up buying a small amount of new stock, and he made a healthy profit over the next six months. He waved newspaper headlines about the rising market in my face and joked about the money I was missing out on by not following the newsletter's advice.

After eighteen months had passed since Ryan had received the first newsletter, he showed me a direct mail solicitation that he had received from its editors. The editors pointed out that they had been giving him great advice for the last eighteen months for free. However, if he wanted to continue receiving this excellent advice in the future, he would have to pay a small subscription fee.

"I'm a satisfied customer, and I'm going to sign up," Ryan said. "I've got to find out whether they think it's time for me to buy or sell. Would you like me to see about getting you on their mailing list?"

"No thanks, Ryan," I said. I thought about telling Ryan that I thought he was making a mistake by putting his faith in the company's predictions, but I bit my tongue. I was reluctant to get involved any further in my friend's financial decisions. I was convinced, however, that in the long run the fee for the newsletter would be a waste of money.

You might think that I was being overly cautious by continually telling Ryan not to follow the newsletter's financial advice. After all, the publication demonstrated a consistent performance over the course of a year and a half, and Ryan had profited by adhering to its guidance. Nevertheless, my natural skepticism told me that the newsletter was bound to fail my friend eventually. When I found some time, I did some thinking about financial newsletters.

Everyone's an Expert

From a critical perspective, here is an example of how these newsletters might work. A publisher creates eight financial newsletters, each of which is managed by a different expert. Each of the eight makes a six-month prediction about the general direction of the market. In their first issues, four predict a rise in the market, and four predict a fall. It turns out that the four who predicted a fall in the market are correct, and these analysts advertise the accuracy of their prediction to subscribers, while the four analysts who predicted a rise in the market immediately go out of business. Of the four newsletters that remain, two predict a rise in the market for the second six-month period, and two predict a fall. When the market rises, the two that predicted a fall go out of business. Of the two publications left after twelve months, one predicts a rise in the market for the third six-month period, and the other predicts a fall. The market rises, and the newsletter that was correct all three times advertises this fact. This, interestingly enough, is the newsletter that was sent to my friend Ryan. The expert appears to have some important insight into financial markets; however, when there are lots of so-called experts making predictions about market performance, some will be consistently correct simply by chance.

Ryan was being too generous in attributing genuine expertise to the editor of the newsletter. When I made this argument to Ryan, he grudgingly agreed that his newsletter's predictions were too good to be true. Besides, he had just lost out on big profits by selling some stock as a result of the newsletter's latest advice.

This assessment of financial newsletters may sound harsh, and any implication that the publishers are deliberately trying to con you is not intended. Keep in mind, however, that there are currently more than *five hundred* different financial newsletters being sold in the United States.[1] If each of these newsletters make three clear predictions on events that have a 50–50 chance of being correct, 62 will have perfect records simply by chance. No evidence has yet been provided that financial newsletters, in the aggregate, perform better than chance. More importantly, there is no known systematic way to predict which newsletters will be more accurate in the future. We can only determine which ones were most accurate in the past.

Mutual Respect

This problem of giving credit to experts based on lucky guesses is not limited to newsletters. Consider another investment—mutual funds. We all read advertisements for mutual funds that have performed well over the last year, making us feel guilty for not having chosen that fund earlier, even though common sense would show that any large family of mutual funds (Fidelity and Dreyfus, for example) will always have some funds that have performed well above the market and some that have performed well below it. However, we only see the advertisements for those funds that have performed above the market. When the above-market funds fall below market, they are no longer advertised.

Consider the following choice. You can select one of the following two options for a 10-year investment:

1. You can invest your money and receive the average return of all stocks less 0.2 percent.

2. You can invest your money and receive the average return of all stocks less 1.2 percent.

This looks like an easy one. Option 1 appears to be a far better investment. The surprising result, however, is that, collectively, the market for mutual funds opts for the second investment over 90 percent of the time. The first option is the decision to buy an index fund. Index funds are passive funds that buy entire markets (for example, the entire Standard and Poor's 500). The Vanguard Index Trust 500 does exactly that (as do many firms that have created index funds). It is guaranteed to perform at the level of the overall market to which it is indexed, minus a small operating fee (0.2 percent in the case of the Vanguard Index Trust 500). Option 2 is the overall performance of all equity mutual funds that were in operation for the entire 1982–1992 period. Of course, Option 2 also requires significant investment of your time to select a mutual fund.

The main reason for the relative success of index funds is that they reduce the expenses of the mutual fund. Other funds have sales fees, operating expenses, and high portfolio turnovers far higher than index funds. In addition, the aggregate set of selections of active funds (where the manager is choosing stocks) is bound to create the market and match the market. Thus, in the aggregate, active funds will match the selections of index funds, but will incur large costs in doing so. Of course, you plan on selecting one of the so-called good mutual funds, and this is possible. A very small number outperformed the Vanguard Index Trust 500. Following are figures for the period 1982–1992:

- 20 out of 205 leading funds had an annual return 5 percent or more below that of the S&P 500.

- 28 out of 205 leading funds had an annual return 3–5 percent below that of the S&P 500.

- 78 out of 205 leading funds had an annual return 1–3 percent below that of the S&P 500.
- 40 out of 205 leading funds had an annual return 0–1 percent below that of the S&P 500.
- 23 out of 205 leading funds had an annual return 0–1 percent higher than that of the S&P 500.
- 13 out of 205 leading funds had an annual return 1–3 percent higher than that of the S&P 500.
- 2 out of 205 leading funds had an annual return 3–5 percent higher than that of the S&P 500.
- 1 out of 205 leading funds had an annual return 5 percent higher than that of the S&P 500.

Now let's assume that you plan on being among the three mutual funds that perform three percent or more above the index. How are you going to get there? Don't forget that other investors who are picking the funds that perform well below average are also intent on picking winners. One of the most common recommendations is to look at past performance. However, John Bogle, Chairperson and CEO of Vanguard Funds, notes:

> Marketers of mutual funds have a fairly easy time achieving—and then bragging about—returns that mark their fund as "#1." Here is the strategy: select a fund that ranks first in any class of funds with similar objectives and asset size . . . over any specified period of time (the past quarter or year or even 25 years). Advertise it as #1. When the ranking subsequently drops (and it will), select another fund . . . and advertise it as #1 . . . These promotions provide simplistic information that is easily manipulated and has absolutely **no predictive** value . . . Similar rankings published in the financial press lack the fund sponsor's bias . . . However, these rankings are also utterly without predictive value . . .[2]

Bogle provides evidence of his very strong claims. For each year in the period 1982–1991, he identified the top 20 mutual funds and assessed how well they did in the following year, consistent with how investors might use this information. Funds in the top 20 out of 681 potential funds in a given year obtained an average rank of 284 out of 681 funds in the subsequent year. This is slightly better than average, but not enough to compensate for the differential expenses of active funds. This data also suggests that a fund's performance over a period of one year has little predictive value.

Perhaps you should look at performance for more than one year. How about a 10-year period? For a group of 309 funds in existence for the entire period 1972–1992, Bogle identified the 20 best performers for the first 10 years, and explored their predictability for the next 10. The results were astonishing in the lack of predictability based on 10 years of performance. The average fund that was in the top 20 in the first 10-year period ranked 142 out of 309 in the next 10 years. While slightly ahead of average, this performance is far worse than buying an index and avoiding expenses. As Bogle notes, "while the average total return of the top 20 funds during the second decade (+14.3%) was above the all-fund average (+13.1%), it fell well short of the return of +16.2% on the unmanaged S&P 500 Index."[3]

Perhaps these results are limited to bull markets when stocks are doing great. Not so! For the first three months of 1997, the average fund investing in diversified U.S. stocks lost 1.98 percent, while unmanaged S&P index funds gained 2.52 percent. The index beat 87 percent of all funds during this period of time.[4]

The average fund performance is also commonly overstated. Not only do families of funds advertise their winners, they also take their losers out of business. Two hundred and forty-two of the 4,555 stock funds tracked by Lipper Analytical Services were merged or went out of business in 1996.[5] These funds were not randomly dropped. These were the laggards and the fund companies were hiding their poor performance. Research shows that average fund performance is actually much lower than what is commonly reported because the dropped funds are not part of the analysis.[6]

How about selecting a portfolio from an investment company managed by all-star portfolio managers? It was tried. From the fund's offering in October 1986 through the close of 1992, Bogle notes, the expected performance advantage of the all-star managers was conspicuous only by its absence. The unmanaged S&P 500 beat the experts by over a percentage point.

No individual who buys an active mutual fund buys it with the expectation that it will do far worse than average. So why do people buy funds that underperform index funds, and why do they not buy index funds instead? The answers to these questions come not from finance, but from psychology. Psychological factors lead even very bright people to make poor decisions that cost them their time, their profitability, and in some cases, their financial future.

The Psychology of Buying Active Funds

The preceding information provides evidence that is readily available from a variety of financial publications, including *Bogle on Mutual Funds*. Recommending index funds, low fees, and low portfolio turnover as long-term investment strategies are not new concepts. I've included this information so you can see why you resist good advice when you see or hear it. I argue that most people have a false belief in their ability to identify better-than-average investments in advance. This belief comes from a variety of psychological sources. I argue that most investors are tragically influenced by a set of psychological biases that have a substantial influence on their wealth. In this chapter, I identify the five key psychological forces that lead investors to make the mistake of believing they can outperform the market.

Overconfidence

Listed below are 10 uncertain quantities. Do not look up any information about these items. For each, write down your best estimate of the quantity. Next, put a lower and upper bound around your estimate, such that you are 98 percent confident that your range surrounds the actual quantity. Respond to each of these items even if you admit to knowing very little or nothing about these quantities.

1. Whirlpool's sales for 1996.
2. Owens Corning's twelve-month earnings decline from 1995–1996.
3. Dell Computer's three-year (1993–1996) shareholder return percentage increase.
4. Nike's share price as of the close of trading February 21, 1997.
5. Apple Computer's twelve-month loss (from 1995–1996).
6. Quaker Oats' 1996 sales.
7. Market value of United Healthcare (as of February 21, 1997).
8. Viacom's 1996 sales.
9. AMR's increase in earnings growth over a three-year period (1993–1996).
10. CIGNA's 1996 profit.

How many of your 10 ranges should surround the true quantities? If you set your ranges so that you were 98 percent confident, you should expect to correctly bound approximately 9.8 or 9–10 of the 10 quantities. Let's look at the correct answers.

1. $8,696,000,000
2. $284,000,000
3. 1150.5%
4. $74.00
5. $867,000,000
6. $5,199,000,000
7. $9,449,300,000
8. $12,084,200,000
9. 120.1%
10. $1,056,000,000

How many of your ranges actually surrounded the true quantities? If you surrounded 9–10, we can conclude that you were appropriately confident in your estimation ability. Most people only surround between 3 (30 percent) and 7 (70 percent), despite claiming a 98 percent confidence that each of the ranges will surround the true value. Why? Most of us are overconfident in our abilities and don't acknowledge the actual uncertainty or randomness that exists in financial decisions.

This overconfidence is manifested in our false belief that we can identify more successful mutual funds than others. Most people overestimate the likelihood that their investments will outperform the market. Why should you be concerned about overconfidence? Because when you select stocks or mutual funds, you are probably overestimating the likelihood of success. In the investment arena, an even more common pattern is vicarious overconfidence. That is, we overestimate the likelihood that our investment advisor will outperform the market.

Optimism

Over the past 12 months, what is the total percentage return of all your investments? How does this compare to the performance of the S&P 500? It is extraordinarily common for people to inaccurately recall their performance. People exhibit a bias related to overconfidence that is called *optimistic illusions*. Once we buy a specific investment, we have a false tendency to overemphasize the reasons that support that investment and to underestimate the risks. This optimistic illusion may be useful to the morale of a salesperson, but it can be dangerous in the hands of an investor.

People tend to believe that their futures will be better and brighter than other peoples' futures. Students expect that they are far more likely to graduate at the top of the class, to get a good job, to obtain a high salary, to enjoy their first job, to get written up in the newspaper, and to give birth to a gifted child than reality suggests. They also assume that they are less likely than their classmates to have a drinking problem, to get fired, to get divorced, to become depressed, or to suffer physical problems.

Investors not only suffer from having optimistic illusions about their investments, but they also hide from any evidence that might lead them to question the wisdom of their investment decisions. Have you ever compared your investment decisions to one of the standard indices available? Most investors do not. Why? They want to protect their right to be optimistic. If you use an investment advisor, have you ever had that advisor provide systematic follow-up information on the recommendations that they made? For most people, the answer is no. I argue that our psychological craving for good news prevents us from taking a hard look at the actual returns we have received on our investments.

Most of the optimism that we describe is unintentional. However, magazines and newsletters do intentionally distort the success of their advice; they often remind you of the wise advice that they provided in the past, but they fail to mention the inaccurate advice. They also provide anecdotal evidence of their success, rather than betting their reputation on their advice by keeping track of it in a systematic manner. After all, if they did not exhibit this optimism, they could not sell their publications.

Interestingly, financial magazines can get themselves into a logical bind. Recently, a personal finance magazine recommended that readers put 50 percent of their portfolio in an index. However, they also advised investors to invest the remaining 50 percent of their portfolio in actively managed funds in order to outperform the market! An interesting question emerges. If the reader believes that the magazine's advice is likely to lead to outperforming the index on the rest of the portfolio, then why use an index? The simple answer is that the arguments in favor of indexing are overwhelming, and the magazine wanted to cover their bets.

Vividness

Vivid events have a greater impact on decision making than more diagnostic, but bland, data. Index funds are boring, mediocre, and uneventful, yet they also happen to be very good investments. Most of us invest based on vivid data. Last year's advertised return, lists of the supposedly best investments, what our friends tell us, and what Peter Lynch says on TV are all more vivid than 10-year performance results. You should avoid being overly influenced by vivid data. After all, financial publications have a vested interest in providing vivid advice in order to get you to buy the publication! Vivid data sells mutual funds, and mutual fund companies are in the business of taking advantage of this bias.

The stock market provides some telling examples of the tendency of investors to overreact to vivid and recent information. After the April 1986 nuclear accident at Chernobyl in the Soviet Union, U.S. investors sold their nuclear stocks, which caused a dramatic fall in prices. However, the real safety of the nuclear systems did not change dramatically as a result of the Chernobyl accident. Similarly, the stock of Union Carbide fell 30 percent within three weeks of the December 1984 tragedy at its chemical plant in Bhopal, India. Few investors stopped to realize that Union Carbide might reach an acceptable out-of-court settlement. It was more salient to imagine Union Carbide being hit with a devastating financial penalty. More rational investors who bought the stock at its low point turned a hefty profit, even before the stock moved up higher as a result of an unsuccessful takeover bid.[7]

Now, what sells magazines and newsletters? The simple answer is vivid advice! "Ten top picks for 1997" . . . "Money Managers who beat the market by 12%" . . . These are headlines that grab our attention. The point is that investors often pay attention to vivid information, and the people who make money from giving advice exploit our bias toward vividness to their advantage. Vivid stories sell investments!

Denying That Random Events Are Random

In basketball, we often think of a particular player as having a hot hand or being on a winning streak. If your favorite player has hit his last four shots, is his probability of making his next shot higher, lower, or the same as the probability of making a shot without the preceding four hits? Most sports fans, sports commentators, and players believe that the answer is higher. In fact, there are many biological, emotional, and physical reasons why this answer could be correct. However, it is wrong![8] An extensive analysis of the shooting performance of players from the Philadelphia 76ers and the Boston Celtics found that prior shot performance did not change the likelihood of success on the upcoming shot. This statistical result has been replicated on many player groups. This finding is one of the hardest for people to believe, but it is true. The reason is that we can all remember sequences of five hits in a row; streaks are part of our conception of chance in athletic competition. However, our minds do not categorize a string of "four in a row" as being a situation in which "he missed his fifth shot." As a result, we have a misconception of connectedness, when in fact, chance (or the player's normal probability of success) is really in effect.

Belief in the hot hand is especially interesting because of its implication for how players play the game. Passing the ball to the player who is hot is commonly endorsed as a good strategy. It can also be expected that the opposing team will concentrate on guarding the hot player. Another player, who is less hot, but is equally skilled, may have a better chance of scoring. Thus, the belief in the hot hand is not just erroneous, but it could be costly if you play professional basketball or, as we will see, if you buy mutual funds.

The most important conclusion is that you should question the predictability of the future from the past. There is a great deal of randomness there, and even more denial by investors. Why? We are all looking for a way to outperform the market and are unwilling to accept that performing at the level of the market may well be a level of performance that we should be happy to accept.

Regression to the Mean

Listed as follows are the 10 largest stock mutual funds as of March 31, 1997, along with their performance for 1995. During 1996, the average return of this group was 18.68 percent. Before reading further, estimate that return for each specific fund in 1996.

Name of Fund	1995 Annual Return	1996 Annual Return
Fidelity Magellan	36.82%	_____
Investment Company of America	30.63%	_____
Vanguard Index 500	37.45%	_____
Washington Mutual Investors	41.22%	_____
Fidelity Growth & Income	35.38%	_____
Fidelity Contrafund	36.28%	_____
Fidelity Puritan	21.46%	_____
American Century–20th Century Ultra	37.68%	_____
Vanguard Windsor	30.15%	_____
Income Fund of America	29.08%	_____

Think about the processes used to answer this problem. Consider the following logical pattern of thought. "The overall annual return was .55 times larger in 1996 than in 1995. Thus, the most logical expectation for 1996 is to simply multiply each 1995 return by .55." This logic, in fact, is a very common approach in responding to this item.

Unfortunately, this logic is faulty because statistical analysis dictates that we must first assess the predicted relationship between 1995 and 1996. This relationship, formally known as a correlation, can vary from total independence (i.e., 1995 performance has no relation to 1996 performance) to perfect correlation (i.e., 1995 performance is a perfect predictor of 1996 performance). In the former case, the lack of a relationship between 1995 and 1996 would mean that knowing 1995 performance would provide absolutely no information about 1996 performance and that your best estimates of 1996 performance would be equal to the average of the group. However, in the latter case of perfect predictability between 1995 and 1996, our initial logic of simply extrapolating from 1995 performance by multiplying by .55 would be completely reasonable. What is the correlation between 1995 and 1996 performance for these 10 funds? The answer is .109. The actual returns are as follows:

Name of Fund	1995 Annual Return	1996 Annual Return
Fidelity Magellan	36.82%	11.69%
Investment Company of America	30.63%	19.50%
Vanguard Index 500	37.45%	22.86%
Washington Mutual Investors	41.22%	20.18%
Fidelity Growth & Income	35.38%	20.02%
Fidelity Contrafund	36.28%	21.94%
Fidelity Puritan	21.46%	15.15%
American Century–20th Century Ultra	37.68%	13.85%
Vanguard Windsor	30.15%	26.36%
Income Fund of America	29.08%	15.23%

Knowing 1995 performance tells you almost nothing about 1996 performance, which is consistent with the arguments provided earlier in this chapter. Most of us have a biased tendency to extrapolate the past into the future, and this should only be done when the correlation between the two is very high. According to John Bogle, in order to understand financial markets, we must first understand the fundamental concept of regression to the mean.[9] While bond returns tend to regress to the prevailing interest rate, common stock returns tend to regress to the average historical long-term rate of return.

Many effects regress to the mean. Brilliant students frequently have less successful siblings. Great rookies have mediocre second years (the *sophomore jinx*). Firms having outstanding profits one year tend to have average performances the next year. In each case, individuals are often surprised when made aware of these predictable patterns of regression to the mean.

Why is the concept of regression to the mean counterintuitive? Individuals typically assume that future outcomes (e.g., 1996 returns) will be maximally representative of past outcomes (e.g., 1995 returns).[10] Thus, we tend to naively develop predictions that are based on the assumption of perfect correlation with past data.

Too Good to Be True?

The Beardstown Ladies, a group of female senior citizens officially known as the Beardstown Business and Professional Women's Investment Club, were able to wow both financial experts and novice investors alike with the high returns that they reported on their investments.[11] They first began to gain notoriety in September 1991 when *CBS This Morning* featured them in a segment on investment clubs. Searching for a kinder and gentler take on Wall Street investing, Gordon Rothman, a producer at *CBS This Morning,* found exactly what he was looking for in the Beardstown Ladies—"a lovely tableau of sweet old ladies saving their pennies for Sunday."[12] Since then, the women have appeared as investing experts on such programs as *20/20* and *Donahue,* and they have been credited with the rise in popularity of small investment clubs. In 1994, there were fewer than 13,000 investment clubs. By 1998, that number had increased to over 34,000.[13] The public was impressed with the success of the Beardstown Ladies and was convinced that if these grandmothers could outperform the market, then so could they.

Their first book, *The Beardstown Ladies' Common-Sense Investment Guide*, came out in January 1995 and has sold over 800,000 copies.[14] In the book, the women claimed to have out-performed the market and to have made a 23.4 percent return on their investments over a 10-year period by following the simple, straightforward strategy of investing in well-known companies such as Coca-Cola, McDonald's, and Wal-Mart.[15] Their second book, *The Beardstown Ladies' Stitch-in-Time Guide to Growing Your Nest Egg*, came out in 1996 and has sold over 400,000 copies. More books, a video, a web site, and countless seminars and speaking engagements have followed.[16]

This great story, however, unraveled in a recent article in *Chicago* magazine.[17] Reporter Shane Tritsch noticed a curious disclaimer on the copyright page of the 1996 edition of *The Beardstown Ladies' Common-Sense Investment Guide*. The disclaimer, which did not appear until the 1996 edition of the book, states that the members' dues were included in the club's annual return figure. It also goes on to state that this kind of return was calculated in a way that is probably different from the way that a return on a bank account or mutual fund would be calculated. In other words, according to the disclaimer, stock appreciation + dividends + monthly dues = the Beardstown Ladies annual returns.[18]

The club's annual dues were around $4,800 for the ten-year period that the book covers. The club was worth about $30,000–$40,000 during some of the years within this decade. In these years, as *Wall Street Journal* reporter Calmetta Coleman points out, if dues were counted as appreciation, the Beard-stown Ladies would have had double-digit growth from dues alone. This, says Coleman, is why the Beardstown Ladies were able to beat Standard & Poor's 500.[19]

When the Beardstown Ladies first heard that their high returns were being questioned, they staunchly defended themselves against the media's accusations.[20] "You can't get the president of the United States, so you're going after little old ladies now," complained a spokesperson for the Ladies.[21] The club's confidence began to wane, however, after they allowed Price Waterhouse to scrutinize their reported returns. The results of the audit revealed that the Beardstown Ladies have had an average annual return of 15.3 percent over the past 14 years of their club's existence. In addition, the audit showed that the club had an average annual return of only 9.1 percent from 1984–1993, the decade covered by the *Common-Sense Investment Guide*.[22] The actual 9.1 percent return was below "the Standard & Poor's 500 average annual return of 14.9% or even the average general-stock-fund return of 12.6% during that same period."[23] The 23.4 percent return rate that the Ladies boasted was true only for the years 1991 and 1992. Betty Sinnock, the club's treasurer, places the blame for the miscalculation on a computer input error, which she says was probably her fault. "I guess we were a group of naïve senior citizens who just felt real good when the computer gave us that return," says Sinnock.[24]

My intention here is not to critique the claims or practices of the Beardstown Ladies. What interests me is the fact that the Beardstown Ladies were accepted by millions of people as legitimate financial experts. While their investments underperformed the market, the royalties from their book sales have more than made up for their low returns. Why did agents, the media, publishers, and most importantly, the public believe their story when a simple check of the data would have proved that their advice didn't live up to the hype? The answer is that investors wanted to believe that the market could be consistently outperformed, and the grandmothers gave them a good story. Optimism led the public to believe the story rather than to check to see if it indeed really was too good to be true.

Advice

This chapter shows that very bright people are currently paying billions and billions of dollars per year for collectively useless advice. People do this for the following five reasons:

1. They are overconfident in their ability to pick funds that will outperform the market.
2. They are overly optimistic about their investments and their financial advisors.
3. They are inappropriately affected by vivid information.
4. They deny the randomness of events.
5. They fail to recognize the principle of regression to the mean.

These five mistakes exist not only in the financial arena, but beyond the context of money as well.

These common errors are easily avoidable. Before making your next investment, evaluate the basis of the information that you are using. Are you paying for random advice? Don't! Are you paying too much to manage your money? Don't! Are you responding to recent vivid data? Don't! However, should you run out and sell all of your current investments? No! Important tax consequences influence these decisions and need to be considered before making any major change to your portfolio. These strategies will be more easily applied to your future investments than to your current ones.

Chapter

7

WHICH JOB OFFER
SHOULD I ACCEPT?
NEGOTIATING WITH
YOURSELF AND LOSING

After earning undergraduate and graduate degrees in photography, Keith suddenly found his years of hard work culminating on one very interesting day. That morning, the owner of a prestigious photography studio called to tell Keith that he had seen some of his photos in a student exhibition, and was very impressed with them. He encouraged Keith to continue his artistic photography, and offered some guidance on developing his artwork further. Keith was on cloud nine the rest of the morning. While he knew that much difficult work would lie ahead and that the likelihood of success was low, the phone call had bolstered his enthusiasm about devoting all

Claire Buisseret provided research and writing assistance on this chapter, and Katie Shonk and Leah Kidwell provided editorial work on its completion. The title for this chapter is borrowed from a related paper by M. H. Bazerman, A. E. Tenbrunsel, and K. A. Wade-Benzoni (1998), Negotiating with yourself and losing: Making decisions with competing internal preferences, *Academy of Management Review, 23,* 225–241.

his energy to an artistic career. Later that day, Keith opened his mail to find a job offer to be a corporate photographer—for more money than he ever imagined he could earn taking pictures. Keith knew, however, that time would not allow him to pursue both the creative life and a corporate career. He would have to choose between the two—and soon. Keith was torn. He wanted to pursue his art, but felt that he should accept the corporate job.

Leigh had been employed by the same company since graduating from college four years earlier. On her twenty-sixth birthday, she got a cake from her coworkers and a call from a woman in the company's benefits division, who reminded Leigh that she was now old enough to enroll in the firm's retirement plan. Naomi explained that the company provided an excellent incentive program, matching any money that Leigh might put into her retirement fund. Leigh told Naomi that she'd stop by her office to pick up the forms. However, in the following weeks, Leigh kept putting off the trip to Naomi's office. She knew that saving for retirement was a good idea, even at age twenty-six. However, putting money into retirement would lower her take-home pay to a level that would put a real cramp in her budget. Leigh had been using her spending money to slowly decorate her apartment, and she had recently seen a sofa at the mall that she knew would be the perfect centerpiece for her living room—for a price of $3,000. Charging the sofa on her credit card would mean slowly chipping away at the debt for months, maybe even years. While Leigh wanted the sofa terribly, she knew that instead she should save for retirement.

These two seemingly disparate situations illustrate the central theme of this chapter: decision makers must frequently choose between what they want (intrinsically) versus what they think (cognitively) they should do. Both examples involve conflicts of choice, in which individuals are motivated to choose between two or more different options at once. These conflicts can create a particularly vexing class of problems because frequently people can be tempted to behave contrary to their best interests.

Having to decide between doing what we *want* to do versus what we think we *should* do is simply a part of daily life. For example, we constantly face decisions about issues that affect our health: whether to exercise, how long to sleep, what to eat, how often to visit the doctor or dentist. In the workplace, we also face constant dilemmas between what we want to do and what we know we should do. Burn the midnight oil to meet that important deadline, or spend the evening relaxing at home with your family? Stay in an enjoyable, low-responsibility position that gives you time for hobbies and vacations, or take a more demanding, stressful job for more money and prestige? Our purchasing behavior is highly affected by want/should choices: buy a cake at a bakery, or save some money and bake it from scratch? Should I drive out of my way to shop at the store that sells "green" paper products and organic vegetables, or stop at the convenience store on the corner and buy whatever they have in stock? Every day we are faced with a bewildering array of want versus should choices. This chapter analyzes this internal conflict, particularly as it affects our finances, and offers a number of remedies.

Split Personality?

As human beings, we are seldom single-minded in knowing what we want and knowing how to get it. When faced with any decision, we can usually think of multiple ways of behaving and multiple desirable outcomes. At the end of the day, when we are trying to decide whether to turn the steering wheel toward the gym or instead head for home, we can think of numerous reasons to go in either direction, each with its own rationale. We experience conflicting desires at the same time—the desire to exercise and the desire to take it easy. Our motivation for going to the gym can be expressed as what we feel we should do, specifically for health reasons. The motivation behind not going to the gym is a much more basic, visceral response—lack of energy, motivation, or desire.

The tendency to want to follow more than one course of action has been described by Thomas Schelling as the "multiple self" problem.[1] We each have in us a *want* self and a *should* self, with each self valuing different outcomes at different times. How do we distinguish between these two selves? One important difference is that our want self is interested in immediate results, while our should self considers long-term results. Since the results or repercussions of most of our decisions are not immediately felt, this difference has strong implications for the choices we make.

If our want self continually dominates our should self, we can become trapped in a destructive pattern of decision making. Maladaptive social behaviors such as smoking, drinking, gambling, doing drugs, and overeating can all be traced to a lack of control over the want self. Many of us have problems with self-control and our management of money. This tendency can lead to more subtle economic behaviors that are equally counterproductive, such as saving money in noninterest-bearing Christmas clubs and giving free loans to the government by overpaying taxes to get a refund.

It takes patience and imagination to plan for the long term. Our should voice is the one that encourages us to methodically visualize what may be. If we focus exclusively on the here and now, we shut out our should voice and refuse to wait. Blocking out our should voice may mean acting against our best long-term interests in favor of short-term solutions. Specifically, people fail to take into account the fact that their wants and desires constantly shift and change. Spur of the moment impulse buys are a perfect example. When faced with the object of your desire, it is easy to forget to thoughtfully assess how you will feel about it a week, a month, a year, or even 10 years from now. When people do not take their changing preferences into account, they are less likely to follow their long-term plans and thus exhibit more impulsive behavior. When people anticipate their changing tastes and adopt strategies to cope with these changes, they are more likely to stick to their plans.[2]

Timing Is Everything

The two selves place different value on different preferences at different times depending on how a decision is framed. These conflicting preferences can make the timing of a decision quite important. When we have one option at a time to consider, we tend to choose what we want. When we have multiple options presented to us at one time, we are more likely to consider what we should do.[3] Having more than one option elicits a more reasoned response. This finding bolsters the advice I gave in Chapters 2 and 3, that it is always a good idea to have several options to choose from when making an important decision. Otherwise, you are liable to be captivated by the persuasive voice of your want self.

To be successful in many professions, you must learn to manipulate salient motivators in others, according to researcher George Loewenstein.[4] Automobile and electronics salespeople and realtors try to play on your immediate, transient concerns in order to sell their commodity. The car salesperson will encourage you to take a test drive so that, out on the open road, you will experience the visceral thrill of driving a brand new car. Realtors know the immeasurable value that fresh-cut flowers, soft classical music, and the smell of brewing coffee can bring to a house up for sale; these props appeal to the prospective buyer's senses, making him or her feel right at home. Other examples are con men who exploit people's desire for a quick buck; state lotteries and casinos can also be accused of resorting to this ploy to a lesser degree. Police interrogators use hunger, thirst, and sleep deprivation to extract confessions;[5] cults have been known to use food deprivation, forced incontinence, and social pressure to overcome long-term self-interest.[6] It is not difficult for people to talk or coerce us into purchasing something that, in the long run, may not be what we really want or need; in fact, it may even be something that is harmful to us. Being aware of salespeople's tricks of the trade will help us avoid becoming their next victim.

Starving Artist or Corporate Sell-Out?

Keith's job choice brings out another important aspect of financial decisions. Keith is influenced by some very salient motivators. As I have explained, our more impulsive want self responds to immediate, visceral emotions or pressures and sways us toward making quick decisions.[7] The joy of taking artistic pictures leads Keith to want to continue pursuing his creative outlet despite the financial hardship that will almost certainly follow. His want response dominates; he is motivated to follow the intrinsically motivating path in life. Frequently, stress or pressure can contribute to our making hasty decisions merely to relieve the unpleasant feelings associated with making a difficult decision, causing us to inadequately evaluate the lasting or permanent effects of our decisions. Under such conditions, the want self is more likely to win than the should self. Thus, this major decision in Keith's life could easily be influenced by the transient influences. He might decide to take the encouraging phone call from the photo studios as the sign he has been waiting for to follow his artistic career.

I want to be clear that I am not arguing that Keith choose the corporate career. Just because Keith is motivated by visceral emotions does not mean that, if he were to choose to pursue his artistic career, he would be making a bad decision. Rather, I believe that he should make a well-informed decision based on a careful assessment of the costs and benefits of each path. Although the want self has a tendency to lead us astray, it also provides a valuable service, which I describe later in this chapter.

The Retirement Dilemma

Another way of differentiating between the two selves is to consider whether they favor temporary or permanent goods. By temporary goods, I mean the money we have in our hand today (or money we can take out of the bank today) and what we can spend it on. A permanent good is our financial well-being when we are no longer working or able to work. Under the influence of the want self, people have a tendency to confuse temporary and permanent goods. For example, people trying to save money will rationalize buying commodities that are temporarily enticing but not essential or useful in the long term, such as Leigh's sofa. Failing to register for her firm's retirement plan would mean literally thousands of dollars in lost funds, money that could make a crucial difference in the quality of her life after retirement, when the $3,000 sofa would only be a hazy memory. In Leigh's case, it should be obvious that letting her want self win would be a far greater mistake than letting her should self get an iron grip on her purse strings. Living a life of debt or having no money for retirement are far more serious problems than dying with money in the bank because you were cheap your whole life. Clear evidence exists that saving for retirement is a good idea, and that too few people follow this guidance. It should be obvious that running up a credit card debt, a pattern Leigh was tempted to begin, will cause you to be able to buy fewer goods in your lifetime as a result of all the money you would have wasted on interest.

So, if the choice is so clear, why do so many people like Leigh fail to save for retirement? We fail to save because the benefits of saving for retirement are only enjoyed many years after we have actually put the money aside. In other words, our decision to put the money aside has to be made many years before we can actually reap the rewards of that decision. Committing ourselves to saving for retirement is a decision that our should self encourages, while our want self tends to be more short sighted, focusing on putting money to use in the present. In reality, we need a balance between the want and should selves. After all, if the should self always wins, we will miss many of the exciting opportunities in life that arise only from acting on impulse.

Which Self Should Win?

In discussing the multiple selves problem, Dick Thaler describes two selves related to want and should: the *planner* and the *doer*. Thaler applies this distinction to contemporary society, and finds the planner triumphing over the doer at Alcoholics Anonymous meetings, drug abuse centers, diet clubs, and smoking clinics. According to Thaler, all of these groups have developed effective methods of controlling the doer, which include:

- Changing the doer's preferences (individuals are taught that exercise can be fun).
- Monitoring the doer's behavior (users submit to drug tests to deter further abuse).
- Altering incentives (alcoholics take the drug Antabuse, which will make them ill if they take a drink).
- Altering rules (dieters outlaw fattening snacks in their home).[8]

While I believe that far more good than harm would come from following Thaler's advice, his ideas are a bit too rigid because they ignore the insight that the want self or the doer can provide. Responding to transient desires is often an adaptive function, serving a valuable signaling role, according to Loewenstein.[9] "Hunger signals the need for nutritional input, pain indicates the impingement of some type of potentially harmful environmental factors, and emotions serve a range of interrupting, prioritizing, and energizing functions."[10] These responses contain information that should not be ignored.

The key question is: Given the number of different voices clamoring in our heads when we are trying to make a decision, to which do we listen? How do we decide on a path that will truly be in our best interest? There are a number of steps that individuals can take to improve their decisions in the face of competing internal preferences.

I believe that the want self may convey important information about emotional criteria that are underweighted because the rational should self cannot explicate them clearly. Perhaps the should self is too conservative, risk averse, or even boring to maximize an individual's self-interest. While the want self may often advocate the least practical choice, it can also provide useful information about our attraction to different options. It adds texture, color, and emotion to the black and white, flat, and rational assessments of the should self.

Returning to Keith's career dilemma, we can well imagine how dissatisfied he would be if he took the job as a corporate photographer and found that he had no time or energy left to pursue his artistic photography after hours. Thus, the joy that his artwork had brought to his life should not be underrated in his decision-making process.

How can we give voice to the want self to improve decisions? I offer two directions; the first comes from decision analysis and the second from research on how to provide rational advice to negotiators.

Decision Theory

Howard Raiffa, a key contributor in the fields of decision making and negotiation, developed the area of decision analysis that outlines how to give prescriptive advice to decision makers. In part, this work formalizes the process in which multiple criteria are identified and weighed. In an apocryphal, ever-changing story, Raiffa, a professor at Columbia University, received an offer from Harvard. He visited a friend, who also happened to be his dean at Columbia, and asked for advice. The dean, borrowing from Raiffa's own writings, told Raiffa to identify the relevant criteria, weight each criterion, rate each school on each criterion, do the arithmetic, see which school had the best overall score, and go there. "No!" Raiffa supposedly exclaimed. "You don't understand—this is a *serious* decision."

While Raiffa pleasantly but forcefully insists this simply is not true, the story is useful for our purposes. The dilemma exemplifies the tension that is always present between the want self (who would make the decision based on gut feeling) and the should self (who would conduct a formal decision theoretic analysis and accept the higher score). This story coaxed Raiffa to clarify exactly what he would do in a situation where conflict existed between the two selves. He urges decision makers to probe each self to find out which one is making the error in judgment. The should self will be able to clarify for the want self that its gut feeling is providing a limited perspective—in other words, it is ignoring the long-term implications of the decision. In turn, the want self will be able to elucidate for the should self some harder-to-identify factor that is missing from the formal analysis.

According to Raiffa, this communication should take place until reconciliation occurs and a clear decision is reached. Disagreement should indicate the need to think more carefully about the information provided by each of the two selves when

100

making important decisions. The decision can be made when the "umpire" self realizes which self (want or should) was neglecting some essential component of the problem.[11] This decision theoretic approach to the multiple selves problem would most likely favor the should self, but would give voice, opportunity, and input to the want self.

Following the decision theoretic advice may lead the want self to rebel against the decision. A diet or exercise regime could be sabotaged by an individual's failure to reconcile the want self to the should self's new agenda.

Our second line of advice grants the want self more autonomy and a stronger voice in the decision-making process by creating a rational negotiation between the two parties (the want and the should selves).

Negotiation Research

It is hard for the different selves to negotiate if they cannot be simultaneously present. If the should self simply tries to control and dominate the want self through rigid, overly restrictive, or punitive decisions, the want self is frequently able to declare an impasse in the negotiation by doing whatever it wants. Everyone can think of instances in which their should self made a decision with the logic of self-interest only to be later overruled by the impulsive behavior of the want self. Do forgotten New Year's resolutions, failed savings plans, and crazed spending sprees ring a bell? For many of us, the list of self-improvement plans sabotaged by the want self may seem endless.

I recommend the development of a rational negotiation strategy for dealing with the want self's insistent cravings. By treating the want self as a negotiator who has the power to declare an impasse and by allowing the parties to negotiate, you will bypass both the domination of the should self in the decision-making stage and the want self in the implementation stage. One could easily argue that this is what occurs naturally. Unfortunately, too often we end up making decisions between the want and should selves in ways that we later regret.

Once we empower the want self in the decision-making process, what criteria should we impose on the negotiation between the selves? First, we would require the parties to reach an agreement, since the independent and conflicting actions of the two selves will inevitably have a worse impact than the result of their collective agreement; a lack of agreement would lead the should self to continue making decisions that are later sabotaged by the want self. Second, the agreement should be such that there is no other agreement that the want self and the should self both prefer over the created agreement. This might consist of discussions and compromises between the two selves about key issues; for example, if your should self puts one quarter of your paycheck in the bank, then your want self should be allowed to propose imaginative (but constructive) ways to spend or invest a portion of the money once it has accumulated. By agreeing to optimal times and limits, the want self is likely to be more willing to follow the agreement. Third, the should self must not push for an agreement that is outside the bargaining zone (see Chapter 2). That is, the should self should not try to reach an agreement on terms that the want self currently or in the future will find unacceptable. The should self must remember that there is no court of law for suing yourself for a contract violation; the want self can void the contract at any time. Thus, if Keith takes the corporate position, there is no guarantee that his want self will perform effectively. If he doesn't create space for his artistic interests, either at his job or in his free time, he will probably become dissatisfied with his career choice. No matter what he decides, Keith must find a balance in his life between his desire for stability and his need to express himself creatively.

Advice

In this chapter, I have proposed two different strategies. My view is that the decision theoretic perspective is preferable as long as the want self does not veto its use. However, if the want self rebels against the terms of the decision, it is probably in the interest of both selves to switch to the negotiation model.

The difficult part of this process is being honest with ourselves about what our concerns and limits are. We need to assess the likeliness that we will do something—either because we want to or because we should. This means recognizing that we will sometimes choose to follow one self rather than the other. When we become cognizant of our wants and shoulds, we recognize the inherent, fascinating duality of human nature. To thoughtlessly succumb to one side is to ignore your own internal complexity. By using techniques such as decision analysis and internal negotiation, you are not only teaching yourself to make wiser financial decisions, you are gaining a deeper understanding of who you are.

These techniques also reduce the likelihood of making the mistakes of thoughtlessly following the want self, or becoming boring by always doing what you think that you should do. In this chapter, I have tried to provide some guidance for auditing how you deal with these two internal voices.

Chapter

8

WHAT'S FAIR AND WHY DO YOU CARE?

Miracle of miracles. After years of listening to the local mega-watt talk radio station give away large sums of money to seemingly every other patient listener in your city, you—you!—and another randomly selected lucky stiff hear your names announced on the air as the winners of a $10,000 jackpot. Deejay Loudmouth Louie has just beckoned you and some other unknown happy camper to call the station within five minutes to claim your shared prize, and you— excited, winning you—heed his summons. Wasting no time, you get on your car phone for your share of the booty, and learn that the other winner, Susan, has telephoned in as well for her cut of the windfall. Knowing the radio ritual, you expect to field a few embarrassing questions with great enthusiasm, maybe force out a few guffaws at Louie's dumb jokes, and then grab the money ($5,000 you presume) and start planning a Jamaican vacation. Life is good.

But then the deejay says something unexpected. For reasons you cannot begin to fathom, Louie tells Susan that she is in charge of dividing up the prize money in whatever way she deems fit, as long as the other winner (you) receives some portion of the jackpot.

This chapter benefited from the research and writing of Amy Binder. Katie Shonk and Leah Kidwell provided editorial and writing assistance.

"Lucky winners," Louie says, "I will give you the $10,000 prize money provided that you two can agree on how to split the cash. In dividing up the sum, you must abide by two rules. First, Susan decides how the $10,000 is to be split between the two of you and then you, Winner Number Two, will decide whether or not to accept the split. If you do decide to accept it, you and Susan will receive the $10,000 based on Susan's division. If you do not accept Susan's split, then each of you will receive nothing. Yes, that's right, nothing. So, whatcha gonna do, lucky winners?"

The stakes are looking a little less rosy than they were just a minute ago, and you realize that you could very well end up with the raw end of the deal. Still, you and Susan agree to play the game. Given the new set of rules, Susan contemplates her options for a second. You are dumbfounded when she says, "I suggest that the $10,000 be split in the following manner. I get $9,900 and you get $100." Your flight to Jamaica has encountered some major turbulence and you're ready to bail. But you can't hang up—the ball is in your court. Will you accept the $100?

If you respond like most people would, you will spurn the split. Why would you do this? Rejecting Susan's deal is not economically rational because each of you would benefit if you accept (a gain of $9,900 for Susan and a gain of $100 for you). But there is an abundance of reasons why you might turn up your nose at this offer.

One reason you might reject this split is because you are ticked off at Susan for putting you in this situation. Here she is with the opportunity to be fair, and instead she chooses to callously look out for Number One. If you do not think about fairness or your emotions, you would probably accept the $100. After all, $100 *is* better than nothing. Furthermore, if the rules of the game were altered slightly, and it was Louie who divvied up the money in the $9,900/$100 allocation, you probably would have accepted the division. What really drives you nuts is that Susan is just another randomly selected player who ought not to have any more control over the situation than you do.

Now, imagine the roles are reversed. You are the one making the decision to split the money, and Susan gets to accept or reject it. What would you elect to do? If you did not take fairness or emotion into consideration, you could easily presume that Susan would accept the $100 (or even less). But this proposal would probably leave you with no money because Susan would be likely to reject it. If you did consider fairness and emotion, however, you could better foresee Susan's probable response, offer considerably more than $100 and increase your shot at making money on the deal.

Or take this example. You walk into a small store and see a simply smashing black leather jacket. It is a must-have, but maybe not at the price the merchant is asking. So you offer him 5 percent over what you figure his cost is on the jacket. He turns you down flat. Five percent over cost still allows him to make money on the transaction, so why does he turn you down? The answer is simple: you have insulted his sense of fairness. A wiser offer would have taken his ideas about what is fair into account. A starting offer of 15 percent over cost might have rattled him somewhat, but he would not have been as offended. And eventually you might have walked out of the door with that great leather jacket on your back—and still at a phenomenal price.

In this chapter, we explore how concerns about fairness affect how we manage money. Specifically, we examine:

- How decisions are affected by our concern about fairness.
- How fairness considerations are affected by framing.
- How social comparison hinder decision making.
- How perceptions of fairness are affected by our relationship with the other party.

Fairness Triumphant: Why We Sometimes Sacrifice Economic Considerations for Fair Outcomes

Because fairness depends on each person's perspective, there is no objective way to judge what is fair or unfair. Even in what we might consider the most clear-cut examples, it is difficult to predict how another person will perceive a situation and decide on a fair outcome. And yet, fairness concerns are crucial for developing a complete understanding of how we make decisions about family and work relationships, as well as many other financial issues. Therefore, it is necessary to understand how fairness considerations enter into our decision-making processes.

For example, there are a number of ways that people might judge whether a situation in which resources are being divided up is fair. A fair outcome might be to allocate resources equally, whereby each party would receive the same amount of the benefit ($5,000 for you and $5,000 for Susan in the example above). A different fair distribution might be to reward each party based on how much effort he or she has put into the situation (a greater share of the $10,000 may be fairly given to you if you tuned into the radio station more often than Susan and could be said to be the more loyal listener). In the business world, this concept is at the root of incentives and merit-based compensation programs. Yet another radically different option is to disburse resources according to the parties' relative needs (say the allocation of the $10,000 is prorated to reflect your and Susan's relative net incomes, and since Susan is a millionaire and only played the game as a lark, she gets very little of the prize). Any of these options could be viewed as fair because each one of us has our own ideas about fairness and will use these ideas in making allocation decisions.

If there is any one area in which we would most like to make completely rational decisions, it is the area of money and other financial matters. But let's think for a moment about one of the fundamental precepts of economic theory and see if we can, in all honesty, fancy ourselves as purely rational actors. The basic principle we will be looking at is the law of supply and demand, a concept that even a person with little schooling in economics is apt to recognize.

A classic research experiment conducted by Kahneman, Knetsch, and Thaler demonstrates that considerations of fairness frequently overshadow purely economic concerns.[1] Imagine that in normal weather conditions a hardware store sells snow shovels for $15. After a fairly severe blizzard, the shopkeeper increases the price to $20. What do you think of his penchant for profit maximization? Is it fair or unfair?

From the perspective of economic action, the price of the shovels should go up. When demand increases relative to supply, a price increase is expected. Despite this purely economic rationale, 82 percent of those participating in the study thought that raising the price of the snow shovels was unfair. And of the 18 percent who said the price increase was fair, many did not think it would be fair to raise the price of generators after a hurricane, even though the logic is essentially the same.

Now, once again, reverse the situation and imagine that you own the hardware store. You've got another twenty shovels in stock. Should you raise their price by $5? Since demand is up for the shovels, if you were to let the market decide what is fair, you could probably make an additional $100. However, if you do raise your price, you may be hurting your future business. Even though you think that your customers ought to understand the laws of supply and demand (and therefore cut you some slack for raising shovel prices), they may decide that your action is unfair and boycott you in the future when they are not at your mercy. That is, if you act in an economically rational manner by increasing the price of the shovels, you may ultimately lose business to your competitors who were wise enough to take the customer's sense of fairness into account in the first place and not raise the price of their shovels. So, even though you may believe that the market is a fair measure of the value of the shovels, you might keep their price steady, resisting the urge to make a few extra dollars, thereby maintaining customer loyalty.

Home Depot, a building-materials retailer, took such wise action on the price of plywood and three other building materials in southern Florida after Hurricane Andrew devastated the region in 1991.[2] Rather than taking advantage of the great need for building supplies, the giant retailer decided to forego sure profits and hold prices at cost plus shipping. In addition to its professed humanitarian inclinations, it is likely that Home Depot was also paying attention to its consumers' sense of fairness. Since these same customers would be around in the months and years following the hurricane, Home Depot could lose profits in the short term in exchange for maintaining customer loyalty over the long term. As testament to the sagacity of this move, one customer declared, "If [Home Depot] had spent $50 million on advertising, they couldn't have bought the good will they got by doing this."[3] For Home Depot, anticipating customers' ideas about fairness proved to be an astute financial decision.

The Effects of Framing: Why Our Sense of Fairness Is Affected by How the Story Is Told

Our sense of fairness is so acute that sometimes we may judge a financial situation as fair or unfair based solely on how the story is told to us, rather than on the facts contained in the story. Consider another comparative problem that the researchers above posed to their survey respondents:[4]

> **Problem A:** A company is making a small profit. It is located in a community experiencing a recession with substantial unemployment but no inflation. Many workers are anxious to work at the company. The company decides to decrease wages and salaries by 7 percent this year.

Respondents answered overwhelmingly that the company should not take this action, with 62 percent saying that the company's behavior was unfair. Now consider the following situation:

> **Problem B:** A company is making a small profit. It is located in a community experiencing a recession with substantial unemployment and an inflation rate of 12 percent. Many workers are anxious to work at the company. The company decides to increase wages and salaries 5 percent this year.

In the second case, just 22 percent of the respondents regarded the company's behavior to be unfair. Even though real earnings remained the same in both scenarios, what people judged as fair was radically different. Because the problem was framed differently, people's evaluations of the company differed too. A small gain that would not even cover inflation was perceived as far more fair than any type of wage cut.

How are we to make sense of this kind of evaluation when, from a purely economic standpoint, it is clearly irrational? It seems that people have rules of fair behavior that are divorced from economic reality. In this pair of problems, for example, it appears as though people believe wages should increase, not decrease, no matter what the state of the economy may be. Therefore, it is very difficult for employees ever to see a pay cut as fair, even when the company's financial condition or the overall economy declines. People think about money in terms of an arbitrary unit (a dollar) instead of in terms of its real purchasing power (real dollars), which is tied to the rate of inflation. That is, they fail to fully realize the influence of inflation on the value of a dollar. People will judge the fairness of wage gains and losses depending on whether they follow the simple rule that wages should go up over time.

Another example of how such general, unstated rules can influence our financial decisions is found in people's preference for equal outcomes. The radio scenario described at the beginning of this chapter demonstrates how this works. Looking at the situation more abstractly, we can better understand what is going on in the minds of Susan and Winner Number Two.

Researchers who have experimented with just such situations have called them "ultimatum bargaining."[5] In a game like this, two players (who are usually strangers to each other) are randomly selected to be either Player One or Player Two. The person conducting the experiment gives Player One a quantity of money (let's say $10) and instructs both players to divide the sum. Player One must propose an allocation, and Player Two must either accept or reject it. If the proposal is acceptable to Player Two, then the money is divided accordingly. If Player Two finds the proposal to be beneath contempt, then neither Player One nor Player Two gets any money at all.

If both players were completely economically rational and decided that all that mattered in the game was the money, then Player One should give the smallest amount possible, say one penny, to Player Two. This proposal ought to be acceptable to Player Two because the gain of a penny is better than no gain at all, which is the result if Player Two rejects the offer. Despite economists' expectations to the contrary, this is rarely how the game is played. Those in the role of Player One very rarely proposed a $9.99/$.01 split. And few Player Ones even proposed a $9/$1 division. You guessed it: a 50–50 split was the most common offer made by Player One. If Player One tried to gobble up too much of the pie, Player Two typically took revenge by refusing to accept, which left both players without winnings. From an economic perspective, a Player Two who turned down *any* amount of money was acting irrationally. But by now we know why this irrationality should be expected, and how it can be explained. Before making a lowball offer (which can be seen as unequal, unfair, and therefore deeply insulting), Player One should recognize that Player Two will be influenced by fairness considerations. This realization would lead Player One to propose significantly more than a measly penny.

Our desire for equality can be so strong, though, that even in cases where Player Two is powerless to protect himself or herself, Player One often proposes fair divisions. In a spin-off of the ultimatum bargaining game called the "dictator game," Player One can unilaterally decide how to allocate the $10, and Player Two has no recourse but to accept the offer.[6] Even under this set of rules, only slightly more than one-third of Player Ones took all the money. Even though Player Two was forced to accept whatever offer Player One came up with, 64 percent of Player Ones in the dictator game gave the other player at least *some* money. The dictator game shows us that people frequently follow some other rule besides the rational economic model when they consider both what is fair and the potential costs of acting unfairly.

Keeping Up with the Joneses: Equality Derived from Social Comparison

There is quite a bit of evidence indicating that people prefer equal to unequal outcomes, no matter what the justification or situation. Another common influence on judgments of fairness is social comparison, or the process of comparing what one person gets to what others receive, even if what the others receive has no bearing on the first person's allotment.

Tim is graduating from a good MBA program. After interviews with several firms, one of the companies he likes best makes him an offer of $85,000 a year. The recruiter is quite clear that the offer is nonnegotiable. Tim likes his potential coworkers, thinks the corporate culture suits him well, and loves the city where the firm is headquartered. "And hey," he proudly thinks, "$85K isn't too shabby." But then Tim makes a discovery that puts a dent in his sense of satisfaction. He finds out that the same company is offering $95,000 to several MBAs graduating from similar caliber schools. Do you think Tim will accept the job offer?

Or consider this situation. Marla gets two job offers that are equally attractive in all areas but salary. The first is from a company that is offering $75,000 to all of its candidates from top business schools. The second offer she entertains is from a company that offers her $85,000, but is known to be offering $95,000 to other MBAs graduating from her very own school. How will she discriminate between these two jobs, and will she let the wages of others influence her decision about where to work?

These offers capture some of the difficulties we find ourselves in when we use social comparison as our yardstick for fairness. Comparisons to other people's situations can create anger, unhappiness, inefficiency, conflict, and missed opportunities.[7] Tim is likely to be deeply bothered by the difference between his salary and the salaries of others, even if he is assured that the beginning difference indicates nothing about how he or his coworkers will be treated in the future. Because he compares his situation to others in order to assess how good his offer is, he may very well pass up an otherwise stellar opportunity.

Interestingly, our research shows that these social comparisons have a profound influence on MBA students in Tim's situation. Yet, the role of social comparison tends to disappear for those in Marla's position.[8] Those with two offers tend to interpret the offers in comparison to one another, while those with only one offer place a great deal of relevance on the salaries of others. The research evidence suggests that when we are evaluating a single option, we place a great deal of weight on social comparisons, but when we have multiple offers, we use the other offers to make sense of each offer under consideration.

A related example is found in the scientific research community, where egos can be big and status comparisons heady. Through its own prodigious efforts at fundraising, a unit of a university medical research lab is given a significant foundation grant to begin innovative genetics research. This money puts the entire lab in better financial shape since scarce resources are no longer required to cover the costs of the genetics unit. In addition, the funding pays for a number of joint capital expenditures (printers, computers, software, etc.), thereby easing the financial crunch experienced by all other units in the lab. Overall, the funding for the research project makes everyone in the entire lab objectively better off, although admittedly some are made more better off than others. This results in anger and unhappiness among members of the lab who are not part of the funded unit. The greater outcomes of the researchers who work on the newly funded project become the arbitrary basis of comparison. The extra resources available to all do not make the lab a more harmonious workplace; instead, jealousy and nonconstructive conflict follow.

The Role of Emotions in Fairness Decisions

Thus far we have talked about people's sense of fairness as if it were a fixed good that remains the same across contexts. But what you might think is fair when haggling with your cousin over the price of his used car may not be what you think is fair when bargaining at a dealership or with a stranger who advertised his car in the classifieds. How do your feelings toward the other person affect your perceptions of what is fair? How do your emotions influence your decision making?

We have noted that people are prone to expect equal allocations of resources in many social situations and business transactions. However, people's tolerance for uneven distributions of resources is also heavily influenced by the type of relationship that exists between the parties. For example, a businessperson involved in a long-term relationship with a client will tend to be interested in the client's welfare, while strangers are less likely to be concerned about each other's outcomes.

The quality of the relationship you have with another person, as well as what the other person receives relative to what you are getting, may de-emphasize the importance you place on maximizing your own outcome. For example, if you like the person you are dealing with *and* that person is receiving only a marginally greater sum than you are receiving, then the unequal allocation may seem more or less fair to you. If one or the other of these conditions does not apply, however, then your sense of fairness is likely to take a nosedive. In one experiment used to test this theory, we asked managers how content they would feel about different money allocations, given different types of relationships with another party: a good relationship, no relationship, or a negative relationship. As we noted earlier, most people prefer equal to unequal allocations in all cases. But if somebody must get the short end of the stick, then managers generally prefer advantageous inequality (where they receive more than the other party) to disadvantageous inequality (where the other party receives more than they do). However, as the relationship with the other party moves from good to bad, the managers become more self-serving in their attitudes toward equal allocation. They become more interested in securing positive payoffs for themselves and are much more likely to prefer advantageous inequality.

Conclusion

This chapter provides an introduction to the cognitive patterns that lead to judgments of fairness or unfairness. A theme of fairness that I touched upon in Chapter 3 (Buying a Car), the psychological role of 50–50 splits, was developed, as were a number of other interesting aspects of how we think about fairness. As you have seen, judgments of fairness permeate our financial life, particularly regarding issues such as pay raises, budgets, promotions, and pricing. While these judgments seriously affect our financial decisions, they are colored by our emotions and behavior and are often not grounded in reality. For example, the degree to which we like and have contact with the people we negotiate with affects our perceptions of how fair a situation is. These factors in turn are influenced by the degree to which resource allocations between parties are equal.

It is not possible to eliminate concerns for fairness and social comparisons from our repertoire; we will always use such information to interpret the world. Rather than trying to smother our biased interpretations of fairness, we should instead view them as useful tools for understanding the reactions that we and other people have to conflicts over money and other valuable resources. Making wise decisions necessitates that you understand the influence of these concerns on your own judgments and decisions, and that you learn to expect that the same sorts of considerations are driving the behavior of others. Neglecting to take these lessons into account makes no more sense than assuming that everyone is completely rational. You need to make money decisions in light of the real emotions and fairness concerns that we all have.

Perhaps the most important part of this evaluation would be an interpretation of the actions of others. We develop our own lens of what would be fair in a given situation, and code it in our own minds as "correct." When others have different interpretations than our own, we often label them as unethical.

The examples in this chapter suggest that disputes can arise between honest individuals as a result of their self-serving interpretations of what is fair. As we saw in the snow shovel example, the seller who focused on economic fairness—the law of supply and demand—outraged buyers who followed a humanitarian model of fairness. Home Depot avoided this conflict by realizing that the fairness concerns of others, even when they ignore economic reality, can provide long-term financial benefits. Clearly, understanding the fairness interpretations of others is an important ingredient in our prescription for avoiding money mistakes.

Advice

I cannot provide you with your value system, nor advise you on the degree to which you should be concerned about fairness. However, I can warn you that our initial emotional reactions are often overly affected by snap fairness judgments.

As you interact with others and try to resolve your money conflicts, bear in mind the following:

- Just as you have your own view of what is fair, so does the person you're dealing with. Be cognizant of the different interpretations of fairness.

- Don't allow your initial emotional reaction to color a decision. When you're making important financial decisions, take time to review and consider how fairness and social comparison biases may be skewing your view of the situation.

9

PUTTING YOURSELF IN THE OTHER GUY'S SHOES

You are traveling in Turkey, a country well known both for its beautiful rugs and for its fierce haggling. You meet a merchant who is selling a gorgeous rug. You have purchased a few expensive rugs before, but you are far from being an expert. Your rough assessment is that the rug is worth about $10,000, but given that your knowledge is a bit rough, you do not want to pay anywhere near that amount. Finally, you make the merchant an offer that you believe is on the low side, though you are not certain.

"I will pay you $1,500 for that rug, but not a penny more," you declare, expecting the haggling to start from that point.

"Fine," the merchant quickly says and begins rolling up the rug. "Will you take it with you or have it shipped?"

You stare at him, dumbfounded that the transaction is already over. How do you feel?

Alex Ooms played a central role in the research and writing of this chapter. Katie Shonk and Leah Kidwell provided editorial assistance.

Most people would feel uneasy about the purchase after such an immediate acceptance. Yet, why would you voluntarily make an offer that you would not want accepted? Certainly, if you were willing to pay $2,000, or even $2,500, you should be thrilled with the $1,500 purchase. So why aren't you? The reason for your uncertainty about your recent acquisition is that you have become a victim of the "winner's curse." The winner's curse occurs as a result of the failure to think about the decisions of the other party and feeling cursed despite winning the deal.

The comedian Groucho Marx once claimed that he didn't want to join any club that would have him as a member. Behind this humorous remark lies a valuable insight. Groucho knew that any club that had standards low enough to accept him was undesirable. If a club allowed Groucho into its inner circle, it would be reducing its attractiveness in his eyes. What Groucho understood sometimes escapes the rest of us: if you make a bid, you need to realize the implications of its being accepted. Groucho realized that being admitted to a club would result in him experiencing the winner's curse.

Of course, not everyone is like Groucho Marx. When some of us join a club, we improve rather than lower its quality. The cable television companies recently learned this lesson courtesy of Bill Gates, chairman of Microsoft. Beginning in 1996, cable companies were entering hard times. In October, *Business Week* featured a cover story titled "Cable TV: The Looming Crises." By May of 1997, despite an overall strong performance in the market, cable stocks were way down, having fallen 21 percent in three months.

In June, however, Bill Gates and Microsoft announced that they were investing $1 billion to buy 11.5 percent of a single cable company, Comcast Corporation. After Gates's announcement, Wall Street took a harder look at the industry and suddenly decided that it was undervalued to the tune of tens of billions of dollars. On the strength of Gates's move, the share price of cable companies—not just Comcast, but companies that had not received any support from Microsoft—jumped by 13 percent in a single week.[1] By admitting Bill Gates to their club, the cable television companies became more valuable to the general marketplace. Gates understood that, unlike Groucho, the implications of his joining the club would be an increase in the value of membership.

Have you ever moved to a new city and been under pressure to buy a house or sign a lease on an apartment within a short period of time? If not, consider this somewhat common dilemma.

Vicki, who lived in Philadelphia, suddenly got an offer with her ideal company, one that she had been trying to find a job with for several years, but they needed her to start right away. The company was located in San Francisco. Between training her replacement, packing up her current apartment, and tying up other loose ends, she only had time for one quick trip out to the West Coast. She knew the housing market in San Francisco was pretty tight, and the company had recommended a real estate agent. After looking at about fourteen houses in two days, Vicki chose her favorite, consulted with the agent, and made an offer at what she believed to be a low price. To her surprise, the offer was accepted immediately.

How did Vicki do? Of course, she did better than if she had placed a higher bid and had that accepted. So why did she feel uneasy when her offer was immediately accepted? Clearly her bid was too high. Where did she go wrong?

Lack of time and unequal information put Vicki at a disadvantage, but failing to think about the information advantage of the other parties compounded her position. Vicki should have realized that the agent, whose pay is linked directly to the selling price of the house, did not have her best interests at heart (see Chapter 2). In addition, the seller had information that Vicki did not have. It is only to be expected that the sellers of houses know more about the market than out-of-town buyers, for they have watched the market for many months.

Vicki would have done better trying to ferret out as much information as possible from the seller, agent, or even better, an independent source. Even then, she would still have to face the inherent information inequality of the situation.

A Quiz on the Winner's Curse

To see if you have grasped the concept of the winner's curse, try your hand at the following corporate acquisition problem, which has befuddled many successful executives:[2]

> You represent Company A (the acquirer), which is currently considering acquiring Company T (the target) by means of a tender offer. You plan to tender in cash for 100 percent of Company T's shares, but you are unsure of how high a price to offer. The main complication is that the value of Company T depends directly on the outcome of a major oil exploration project it is currently undertaking. Indeed, the very viability of Company T depends on the exploration outcome. If the project fails, the company under current management will be worth nothing—$0 per share. But if the project succeeds, the value of the company under current management could be as high as $100 per share. All share values between $0 and $100 are considered equally likely. By all estimates, the company will be worth considerably more in the hands of Company A than under current management. In fact, whatever the ultimate value under current management, *the company will be worth 50 percent more under the management of Company A than under Company T.* If the project fails, the company is worth $0 per share under either management. If the exploration project generates a $50 per share value under current management, the value under Company A is $75 per share. Similarly, a $100 per share value under Company T implies a $150 per share value under Company A, and so on.

The board of directors of Company A has asked you to determine the price they should offer for Company T's shares. This offer must be made *now*, before the outcome of the drilling project is known. From all indications, Company T would be happy to be acquired by Company A, provided it is at a profitable price. Moreover, Company T wishes to avoid, at all cost, the potential of a takeover bid by any other firm. You expect Company T to delay a decision on your bid until the results of the project are in, then accept or reject your offer before the news of the drilling results reaches the press.

Thus, you (Company A) will not know the results of the exploration project when submitting your price offer, but Company T will know the results when deciding whether or not to accept your offer. In addition, Company T is expected to accept any offer by Company A that is greater than the (per share) value of the company under current management.

As the representative of Company A, you are deliberating over price offers in the range of $0 per share (this is tantamount to making no offer at all) to $150 per share. What price offer per share would you tender for Company T's stock?

My tender price is: $ _____ per share.

This exercise is logically similar to the rug story and to Vicki's house purchase. Groucho's insight helps us solve all three problems. In the acquisition exercise, one firm is considering making an offer to buy out another firm. The acquirer is uncertain about the ultimate value of the target firm, and only knows that its value under current management is between $0 and $100 per share, with all values equally likely. Since the firm is expected to be worth 50 percent more under the acquirer's management than under the current ownership, an initial analysis suggests that it makes sense for a transaction to take place. While the acquirer does not know the actual value of the firm, the target knows its own current worth exactly.

While the problem is analytically quite simple (as will be demonstrated shortly), it is intuitively perplexing. The response that MBAs, CEOs, accounting firm partners, and investment bankers typically give ranges between $50 and $75 per share. The most common (but wrong) thought process that leads to these answers is that, "*on average,* the firm will be worth $50 per share to the target and $75 per share to the acquirer; consequently, a transaction in this range will, *on average,* be profitable to both parties." This logic would be rational if the other side (the target) also only had distributional information about its value. However, you know that the target knows its true value before accepting or rejecting your offer.

Consider the logic that a rational thought process would generate in deciding whether to make an offer of $60 per share.

If I offer $60 per share, the offer will be accepted 60 percent of the time—whenever the firm is worth between $0 and $60 per share to the target. Since all values are equally likely, between $0 and $60 per share, the firm will, on average, be worth $30 per share to the target when the target accepts a $60 per share offer, and will be worth $45 per share to the acquirer, resulting in a loss of $15 per share ($45–$60 per share). Consequently, a $60 per share offer is unwise.[3]

The same kind of reasoning applies to *any* positive offer. On average, the acquiring firm obtains a company worth 25 percent less than the price it pays when its offer is accepted. If the acquirer offers $X per share (you can substitute your offer, X, as we analyze the problem) and the target accepts, the current value of the company is worth anywhere between $0 and $X per share. As the problem is formulated, any value in that range is equally likely, and the expected value of the offer is therefore equal to $X divided by 2. Since the company is worth 50 percent more to the acquirer, the acquirer's expected value is $1.5(\$X/2) = 0.75(\$X)$, only 75 percent of its offer price. Therefore, for any value of $X, the best the acquirer can do is not to make an offer ($0 per share).

It is possible to make money by making an offer on the firm, but you are twice as likely to lose money as you are to gain it. The paradox of the "Acquiring a Company" problem is that even though in all circumstances the firm is worth more to the acquirer than to the target, any offer above $0 per share leads to a negative expected return to the acquirer. *The source of this paradox lies in the high likelihood that the target will accept the acquirer's offer when the firm is least valuable to the acquirer— that is, when it is a lemon.*[4]

The answer to this problem is so counterintuitive that even people who were paid according to their performance exhibit the same pattern of mistakes. Readers of this book have the analytical ability to follow the logic that the optimal offer is $0 per share. Yet without assistance, most individuals make a positive offer. Individuals systematically exclude information from their decision processes that they have the ability to include. They fail to realize that their outcome is conditional on acceptance by the other party, and that acceptance is most likely to occur when it is least desirable to the negotiator making the offer.

Real-World Markets

As many people will tell you, as soon as you drive a new car off the dealer's lot it loses up to 20 percent of its value. The reason for this is the lemon dilemma. Imagine that you answer an advertisement for someone who wants to sell a car that she bought just three months ago for $21,000. She even has the original receipt. When you ask why she wants to sell it she says she is suddenly moving to South America. You are wary, though, because a coworker told you a story about his in-laws buying a used car without knowing that it had been involved in a bad collision and had suffered a damaged axle. The seller had been able to cover up the damage from the accident with new bodywork, your coworker had told you. Suppose that if the car is undamaged it is worth almost full price, or $20,000. If the owner has a valid reason to sell it, she will be willing to accept a little less, or anything over $18,000. So if the car is in good condition it should fetch a fair price of between $18,000 and $20,000. However, let's say that the car was in an accident or is a lemon, and that it would take about $8,000 to restore it to good condition. In this case, it is worth only $12,000, and any buyer that knew the car was a lemon would refuse to pay more than that amount for it. Imagine that there is a 70 percent chance the car is good, and a 30 percent chance that it is a lemon. Without knowing if the car is reliable or if it is a lemon, what would you offer for it? Well, you might offer the expected value: 70 percent of the $20,000 if it is good ($14,000) plus 30 percent of the $12,000 if it is a lemon ($3,600), for a total of $17,600. Does the owner sell you the car? Since it is worth $18,000 if it is good and $12,000 if it is a lemon, she only agrees to sell the car if it is a lemon.

The problem here is simple. The presence of lemons in a market makes it hard for the seller to get full value for high-quality items. George Akerlof analyzed this problem in his classic paper on lemons using the following logic.[5] As the preceding example has illustrated, used cars vary in their reliability, yet most buyers cannot see the difference between a good used car and a lemon. As a result, both reliable and unreliable used cars will sell for very similar prices. Sellers of better-than-average cars will not be able to obtain a price reflective of the true value of their car and thus may choose not to sell their car. As the more reliable used cars disappear from the market, only the worst used cars will be sold at prices that reflect their quality. Where do the good cars go? People keep them longer and sell them to friends and relatives. As a result, the average used car on the market is a below average used car. Akerlof's arguments explain the fall in price as cars leave the showroom.

Solving the Winner's Curse

The Akerlof argument would tend to predict that we would not see as many used goods for sale as we actually do. There are a number of reasons why used markets continue to exist at high levels of volume. First, buyers do not make the inference that the seller of the car (or motorcycle, computer, etc.) that they are considering selectively chose to sell the car. Thus, many buyers continue to make offers without an awareness of their information disadvantage, and suffer the winner's curse. In addition, sellers of high- (or reliable-) quality goods and services can use a number of mechanisms to counter the concerns of buyers about purchasing a low-quality good or service. Car dealers provide customer guarantees, and large organizations work hard to maintain a good reputation so that you will trust their goods or services. For example, travelers are more likely to stay at a hotel chain rather than an independent hotel or inn when visiting a city that they do not know well. Why? The reputation of the brand name gives travelers some confidence in the level of service that they can expect.

Obviously, an ongoing relationship between parties can also solve the winner's curse, since the seller will not want to harm the relationship by taking advantage of the buyer. This is why relatives and friends often buy used cars from each other. Many companies set up bulletin boards where employees can list items for sale not only to save advertising costs, but to improve the buyer's confidence about the true value of the commodity. There are many costs to a seller if word gets around the company that she sold a fellow employee a lemon.[6] The winner's curse can also be solved by a guarantee, given you have a certain amount of time to return the item. If you are planning to use a company's goods or services often, let them know this. Sellers will be less likely to sell you a lemon if they know you intend to come back. You should also be sure to meet with the other party face-to-face. People are less likely to be victimized by the winner's curse in face-to-face interaction than in written communication.[7] Our argument is that most people avoid telling direct lies face-to-face, but are happy to allow you to reach a false conclusion on paper. Thus, I recommend that you meet with the seller and ask very direct, concrete questions about your prospective purchase. In addition, government intervention can also help solve the winner's curse problem. To protect consumers and promote trade, some state and local governments have enforced "lemon laws" in the used car market.

Perhaps the most important weapon in combating the winner's curse is an awareness that people undervalue the importance of getting accurate information when making important transactions. We undervalue a mechanic's unbiased evaluation of a used car, a professional inspector's assessment of a house, or an independent rug expert's assessment of a coveted rug. To protect yourself as a buyer, you need to develop, borrow, or buy the professional expertise necessary to balance the inequity of information between you and the seller. This notion is uncomfortable to many consumers, who do not like paying for something (an appraisal) that will probably reconfirm what they already believed to be true; they feel as if they paid valuable money for nothing. Home buyers argue that the house will be appraised by the bank later in the buying process, failing to realize that that appraisal focuses on the security of the bank's investment, not the wisdom of the buyer's purchase. A more subversive reason that people discount or fail to obtain estimates from third parties is that they have a bias against searching for information that disconfirms their expectations.[8] They may not want to believe that they could have grossly misjudged the value of an item, or they may already be so attached to the item that they are actively avoiding any suggestion that it is less than the perfect bargain. An independent appraisal should not be viewed as an inconvenience, but as insurance against a car that is a lemon, an overpriced house, or a pile of wool masquerading as a valuable rug. The appraisal will typically save you time and money.

Conclusion

People who think more about the perspectives of others are more successful in negotiation simulations, as this focus allows them to better predict their opponent's behavior.[9] Yet most individuals fail to consider adequately the other party's point of view.[10] Unfortunately, people tend to act as if their opponents were inactive parties and systematically ignore valuable information that is available about their decisions.

I frequently give advice to corporations facing important negotiations. After analyzing the specifics of the situation, I often suggest that the negotiators role-play the meeting with the other side to ferret out potential problems before they pop up at the negotiation table. Interestingly, this very effective advice is counterintuitive to important decision makers, who are not used to systematically thinking about the decisions of others. Having each bargainer verbalize the viewpoint of the other party increases the likelihood of a negotiated resolution.[11] Similarly, having individuals play the role of the seller in the "Acquiring a Company" problem increases the likelihood of rational action when they are switched to the role of buyer.[12] This role switching helps people focus on their adversary's decisions.

A critical characteristic of the winner's curse is that one side often has much better information than the other side; that party is usually the seller. Though we are all familiar with the slogan "buyer beware," we often fail to put this idea into practice when the other side has better information than we do. We realize this fact only after buying a commodity we know little about; our uncertainty increases as a function of the other party's acceptance. Rigorously searching for information that disconfirms the value we have placed on a commodity will ensure that, unlike Groucho, we are proud to belong to the clubs that would have us as a member.

Advice

Next time, you're in an important negotiation, remember:

- Role-play ahead of time and try to anticipate the goals and sticking points of the other party.
- Get as much advance information as possible. For example, when you're making any major purchase, you may have to get an expert's (appraiser, inspector, etc.) evaluation. Assume all information may be important. Once you have it, you will be better prepared to negotiate.
- Before shaking on a deal, familiarize yourself with possible solutions to the winner's curse, such as guarantees and so-called lemon laws.

10

KNOWING WHEN TO QUIT

It was Robert Citron's big break. The California native had left college a few requirements short of a degree, and his only financial experience had been as an officer for a company that went bankrupt. So when Citron was offered a job in the Orange County treasury office in 1960, he didn't want to strike out a third time. For the next ten years, Citron worked long hours, and his hard work paid off. He was promoted to supervisor, and, when the treasurer retired, Citron ran for the empty post and won.

Responsible for investing billions of dollars in revenues from almost two hundred public bodies, Citron brought in an astonishing average return of 10 percent per annum during his early years as treasurer. His success attracted praise and honors from the media and from his peers in county management. In a show of gratitude and good faith, the county's Board of Supervisors granted Citron more freedom and less accountability than past treasurers.

Always on the lookout for ways to increase his latitude as an investor of public funds, Citron began lobbying the California state legislature in the early 1980s for the relaxing of statutes restricting county treasuries. His efforts allowed him and other state officials to invest in some of the intriguing financial instruments that were

Katie Shonk provided research and writing support for this chapter. Leah Kidwell provided editing assistance.

emerging, such as reverse repurchase agreements. Surrounded by a close inner circle of trusted advisers, Citron kept the coffers of the Orange County Investment Pool (OCIP) full. The region prospered. Property and sales taxes remained low and community services flourished.

But even as his rocky beginnings became a distant memory, the secret of Citron's success became increasingly mysterious. His annual reports to the Board of Supervisors were vague and simplistic. How was he managing to rack up such huge assets? Why would someone with such great success be so secretive and guarded about his means of achieving it?

For twenty-four years, Citron successfully fended off skeptics, letting his stellar record speak for itself. He ran unopposed in six elections. When a municipal accountant named John Moorlach challenged him in the election of 1994, Citron was shocked and offended. Who dared to criticize the hero of Orange County and on what grounds?

In interviews with the national press, Moorlach warned that Orange County's leveraged investment pool hinged dangerously on interest rates, which had begun to rise precipitously. Refusing to reveal the details of his contingency plans, Citron insisted that secrecy should be an essential component of an investor's strategy. He went on to win the election with hardly any damage to his reputation. In his annual report to the Board, Citron admitted that he had failed to predict the rise in interest rates but insisted that the county's funds were in no real danger.

Despite the election victory, Citron's inner circle found their leader shaken by his opponent's attacks and withdrawn from the increasingly grim financial news. As interest rates began to eat up the county's assets, just as Moorlach had predicted, Wall Street banks and brokerage houses refused to extend the county's loans. Many employees at the county's treasury office began to face the possibility that the OCIP could be facing monumental losses. Meanwhile, Citron began working shorter hours to avoid the turmoil. One coworker even discovered that Citron had begun to consult psychics and astrologers at work.

In December 1994 the bomb dropped on Orange County. The

OCIP, which had seemed bulletproof for over two decades, was facing losses of $1.7 billion. Banks and other creditors were lining up to collect on their loans, but interest rates had cleaned out the pool. The county filed for bankruptcy, and Robert Citron, unable to hide from the truth any longer, tendered his resignation, leaving his office in disgrace.

Many readers will be familiar with the story of the rise and fall of Robert Citron, the treasurer of Orange County who was held largely responsible for the staggering losses suffered by that county in December 1994.[1] In the years since the bankruptcy, Orange County has struggled to recover. Housing prices fell an estimated 5 percent, local school systems have had difficulty making ends meet, and residents have grappled with raising a variety of taxes to cover the losses.[2]

Could one man really be responsible for the loss of $1.5 billion in public funds? And if so, why did no one stop him? These questions are still being hashed out in the courts. On its most basic level, the bankruptcy resulted from Citron's free-wheeling experimentation with derivatives. His high-risk investments paid off for years, and then suddenly, perhaps even predictably, crashed. Citron, however, was hardly the only party responsible for the fiasco. Most notably, Orange County sued Merrill Lynch for $2.4 billion for "wantonly and callously" selling extremely risky securities to the county;[3] Citron worked closely for a number of years with one of Merrill's top salespersons, an advocate of derivatives. In addition, the county's auditors failed to draw attention to Citron's risky investment style, and the Board of Supervisors allowed itself to be hoodwinked year after year by the "magic act" that had kept returns so amazingly high.

Most of us will never have the responsibility of managing a multibillion dollar investment pool. We have all been in decision-making situations, however, where either smaller amounts of money or goods were at stake. Therefore the plight of Orange County offers some valuable lessons about an important judgment bias: the irrational escalation of commitment.

Somewhere over the Rainbow

Escalation situations begin when an individual or group makes a decision for which they are personally responsible. These decisions often reveal our ambitions and goals, however big or small. An entrepreneur pursues a lifelong dream of opening a five-star restaurant. An airline commits to a strategy of cutting costs to win industry price wars. Robert Citron wanted to be the man responsible for bringing prosperity to Orange County. In each case, a person or group makes an initial commitment based on a vision of the future.

In real life, success seldom comes easily. Often we find that, after making the decision we hope will solve all of our problems, things do not proceed as smoothly as we had planned. The new restaurant owner finds that, after the initial buzz, he or she has trouble attracting new customers and quickly loses money. The airline cuts costs so deeply that it begins to receive negative publicity and loses customers who are concerned about safety. Once you have faced a setback resulting from your initial decision, what happens next? Whether you think about it consciously or not, you are now confronted with another decision. Should you continue to remain committed to your goal (via more time, money, and effort), pursue a different route, or abandon the goal entirely? Should the restaurant owner close up shop or take out loans to support advertising and marketing campaigns? Should the airline reexamine the effect of its policy on safety or defend it against press attacks?

Changing course midstream means admitting that your initial decision was less than perfect and facing the loss of everything you have invested so far. Naturally, withdrawing from the situation is not an appealing option. But if you stick to your original plan, will you just be wasting more precious resources?

Robert Citron maintained an appearance of prosperity in Orange County for many years through his elaborate use of smoke and mirrors. Citron actively campaigned for the freedom to broaden his speculative investments by lobbying both the county board and the state legislature. When property values began to fall in the early 1990s, thereby reducing tax revenues, the county began to rely even more heavily on the income from Citron's baby: OCIP. With the very future of the county resting in his hands, Citron indulged in more and more questionable investment strategies.[4]

Had Citron changed course, and decided to try a more conservative approach to managing Orange County's precious savings, he undoubtedly would have disappointed a great number of people. He was the county's miracle worker. If investment returns had suddenly dropped from 10 percent to 6 percent, he probably would have been viewed as a failure, even though most municipal treasuries manage to survive quite well on such modest returns. Citron was obliged to continue delivering the big bucks, even if it meant risking everything he had gained.

The Fork in the Road

The comedian W. C. Fields is attributed with quipping, "If at first you don't succeed, try, try, again. Then quit. No use being a damn fool about it." The trick is to recognize when your persistence in following a predetermined course of action will pay off and when it is simply misdirected. Misdirected persistence leads to an *irrational escalation*, which occurs when we follow a selected course of action that we would not have chosen if we had rationally analyzed our situation. While most of the biases we have looked at so far prevent us from reaching an optimal outcome in an isolated decision, the tendency to irrationally escalate commitment emerges over time.

More often than not, we remain committed to an initial decision, continuing to allocate resources that support it.[5] We may not even consider the possibility of abandoning commitment since sheer inertia can compel us to blindly pursue an impossible goal. Why do we remain focused on the past rather than the future? The dissonance created by our unsatisfactory outcome is disturbing to us; we took responsibility for a decision that has led to a degree of failure—that is, lost money, lost time, or even lost self-respect or reputation.[6] Rather than admit to this failure and attempt to remedy it, we will try to deny its existence by making an even stronger commitment to our initial decision. The greater responsibility we feel for a given decision, the more biased we will be toward committing to this responsibility with subsequent decisions.[7]

Robert Citron irrationally committed to risky investments because, year after year, his luck held strong. His luck led to arrogance, and his arrogance led to a sense of invincibility. In 1993, when asked to explain his belief that interest rates would remain low, Citron replied, "I am one of the largest investors in America. I know these things."[8] Given that soaring interest rates led to Orange County's downfall in the following year, Citron's response sounds ridiculous in retrospect. But in 1993 Orange County citizens did not second-guess the financial genius who had kept the county prosperous for over two decades.

Risky Business

"There's nothing worse than a gambler who goes to Vegas and wins for the first time," said an Orange County political activist, speaking of Robert Citron.[9] Like the novice gambler,

Citron hit paydirt the moment he took his first big risk, and when it paid off, he upped the ante. Now imagine the same Las Vegas gambler who, following his big winning streak, suddenly finds himself losing fast. Determined to win back his earnings, the gambler throws more and more chips onto the blackjack table and, again and again, watches the dealer sweep them away. The gambler, imagining the big-screen TV he had planned to buy with his winnings just minutes ago, continues to hold out hope that his luck will turn with the next hand. However, the dozens of thriving casinos in Las Vegas are proof that most gamblers walk away from the table as losers, and the hundreds of pawnshops that feed off the casinos are signs of the disaster that befalls those who do not know when to quit.

Orange County's bankruptcy and gambling are extreme examples of commitment to a chosen course of action, yet most escalation situations do involve a degree of risk. Entrepreneurs are continually faced with the choice between committing to their venture or cutting their losses. Salient examples of success stories in the media romanticize self-made men and women who started billion-dollar industries on a shoestring. While the downfall of formerly successful conglomerates make the front page, we seldom hear about the thousands of small businesses that go bankrupt after battling a series of disabling setbacks. Even seemingly safe decisions, such as accepting an attractive job offer or placing a bid on a beautiful house, lead to future, less certain decisions. If, after a year, your job starts looking like a dead-end, do you work longer hours to curry favor with your boss, or do you revise your resume? What if you get into a bidding war over your dream house? Will you be able to stop yourself from offering a higher purchase price than you can afford?

Perhaps these pessimistic scenarios make me sound overly cautious and risk-averse. It may seem as if, in asking people to reconsider the way they are approaching their goal or dream, I am advising them to pursue the safe, boring, well-traveled route rather than the more interesting, yet risky, road less traveled. On the contrary, I do not advocate either total risk or caution, but rather a rational and balanced analysis of both options—a third road, if you will.

As a first step toward determining whether to escalate commitment to a given decision, consider the advice of accountants and economists, who remind us that the time and expense we have already expended are *sunk costs*. That is, our past effort is irrecoverable and should not be considered in future courses of action; instead we should reexamine the best outcome we could hope to achieve at this point in time with the resources that remain. By believing that our sunk costs are recoverable, we are overly optimistic about our own abilities and our immunity from unforeseen setbacks.

Why Do We Escalate?

Once you acknowledge that, as a member of the human race, you are highly susceptible to irrationally escalating commitment, you are ready to overcome this tendency and make more rational and sound decisions. This process involves understanding the psychological factors that bias our perception and judgment, recognizing these biases in our own behavior, and learning ways to combat them.

Perceptual and Judgmental Biases: Seeing the Blind Spots

Imagine the reaction of the members of the Orange County Board of Supervisors after they learned that Robert Citron was at least partially responsible for losing $1.7 billion and bankrupting the county. Suddenly, they were confronted with the truth they had been avoiding. They had been wrong to allow

Citron unbridled freedom over the county's investments for the past twenty-four years. Looking back, members of the board remember Citron's rambling annual reports, his defensiveness and secretiveness, and his unbelievably high success rate. Why did they not see these warning signs? The board fell prey to a common bias called the *confirmation trap*. Once we make a tentative decision, in this case, to grant Citron unprecedented independence from the board, we will search for information that supports and confirms the decision, and will fail to search for data that challenges or contradicts it. Dazzled by Citron's balance sheets, the board erred by not recognizing that success must necessarily come with a certain amount of risk.

The best way to avoid the confirmation trap is to diligently search for disconfirming evidence to supplement the confirming evidence that comes to you more naturally. A healthy dose of skepticism would have convinced the Orange County board that even a high performer like Citron should be subject to checks and balances rather than left to his own devices. In most cases, seeking the advice of an impartial third party can be a valuable means of evaluating your decisions. However, be careful! You want to get your information from third parties that do not have an incentive to see you irrationally escalate.[10]

In addition to limiting your perception, your first decision will also bias any subsequent decisions that you make. If the board had not felt responsible for granting Citron great control over the OCIP, it would have been more likely to examine his annual reports more thoroughly and to investigate criticisms of him made by financial experts. When faced with Citron's request for more authority, the board considered his high returns and disregarded the possibility that these returns could have been achieved at enormous risk. By recognizing its commitment to Citron as a sunk cost, the board could have considered other alternatives besides immediately accepting his demands.

Impression Management: Is Image Everything?

Citron's risky strategies were advocated by some parties and ignored by others, but very few challenged them. A big factor in Citron's decision to commit to derivatives and other complicated financial transactions was evidently the fear that, if he stopped using them, he would have to account for the lower returns that would inevitably result from more conservative strategies. Similarly, all five of the Orange County supervisors backed Citron in the 1994 election, ignoring the prophetic warnings of his opponent, John Moorlach.[11] People, and perhaps especially success-oriented Americans, hate to admit failure. Acting against an initial decision means admitting, often publicly, that the first course of action was, in some sense, a failure.

Research shows that we prefer leaders who act consistently rather than those who switch from one way of behaving to another.[12] Presidents Carter and Clinton are two recent leaders who at times have come under fire for waffling on the issues. The public's demand for consistency can be damaging, however, because while indecision in its extreme can indeed be disastrous, committing to bad decisions is an equally undesirable leadership quality.

After our first decision turns out badly, we may knowingly continue to make bad decisions simply out of a desire to appear consistent. The U.S. savings and loan (S&L) crisis of the late 1980s is a prime example of this tendency. Politicians unwisely allowed S&L executives to take gambles with taxpayer-insured investments. As the losses mounted, politicians who were primarily concerned with appearing consistent to the public continued to escalate their commitment to the S&Ls rather than admit to their initial mistake. When the scale of the disaster was exposed to taxpayers, it became clear that the politicians would have done well to halt the S&Ls' irresponsible behavior in its early stages rather than quietly condone it in an effort to save face.

This desire to appear consistent and hide past mistakes leads to an interesting double bind for organizational decision makers. They will be acting in their organization's best interest if they make decisions based on objective considerations of costs and benefits rather than on past commitments and sunk costs. This strategy, however, will sometimes lead them to stray from past decisions, thus creating an image of inconsistency. Just as we selectively perceive evidence to support our decisions, we selectively provide confirming evidence to others.[13] It is the responsibility of your organization to build compensation systems that reward good decision making rather than slick impression management.

Competitive Irrationality: When Is a Winner a Loser?

Escalation of commitment does not occur in a vacuum; many outside factors may lead a person to stubbornly hold to a given decision. Even when we have overcome internal biases such as the confirmation trap and impression management, external competition can lead us to escalate irrationally. The $20 bill auction described in Chapter 1 is a classic example of the competitive escalation paradigm. Once two players get locked in a bidding cycle, it becomes difficult for either one of them to admit defeat and both usually end up facing embarrassing losses.

Competing companies often get locked into real-life versions of the $20 bill auction. Two gas stations located at the same intersection may each try to drive the other out of business by lowering the price of its gas. Even if one of them succeeds in knocking down the competition, the cost of victory for the winner will most likely be crippling. The airline industry reached a desperate situation in 1992. Following American

Airlines' introduction of its "value pricing" plan, rival carriers competed to offer the lowest fare to consumers, resulting in such low fares that making a profit became impossible. Also, in the telecommunications industry, AT&T, MCI, Sprint, and smaller long-distance companies have learned that price wars create too much "churn" within the industry. Once consumers switch carriers, the cost of winning them back cuts deeply into the profits gained by luring new customers.[14]

Competitive escalation can be applied to many conflicts throughout the world. The Russian government's commitment to crushing the sovereignty movement in Chechnya escalated for almost five years despite vague objectives, lack of support from the Russian people, low morale among the troops, and a series of humiliating defeats. The conflict, which has been put on hold until the year 2001, led to massive loss of human life on both sides and contributed to the dismal economies of both countries. The Vietnam War is another extreme example of the competitive escalation paradigm.[15]

Advice

To avoid being trapped in a downward competitive escalation spiral, you must acknowledge that there are very few winners in these situations. The best policy is to avoid entering them altogether while finding other ways to maximize your advantage in the marketplace. During the airline or long-distance price wars, for example, a company that vowed to match its competitors but refused to lower them to new levels might have effectively stemmed the downward price spiral. By focusing on your goal rather than on winning at any cost, and by developing innovative strategies to meet that goal, you will be less likely to commit to a situation that may be entirely beyond your control.

When you choose to escalate commitment to a decision, judgmental and perceptual biases, impression management, and competitive irrationality may all be interfering with your ability to make rational choices. By dissecting the motivations behind your actions, you will be able to eliminate your biases and make a series of confident, rational, and perhaps even inconsistent decisions. I do not mean to imply that your gut instinct is necessarily wrong, or that you should avoid risk at all cost and only make seemingly safe decisions. Rather, I advocate well-informed risky decisions *if* you accept the possibility that the decision will turn out badly, and if you are prepared to change course midstream. This means you must:

- Maintain a vigilant assessment of your past actions.
- Recognize minor failures before they become catastrophes.
- Implement swift and innovative solutions.

11

PLAYING TO WIN

It had all fallen apart. After spending ten years together in holy matrimony, through thick and thin, for better and for worse, here they were in her lawyer's office trying to hammer out the grisly details of their divorce. Given the ugliness of the current proceedings, it certainly didn't feel like it ever could have been "holy," "thick," or "better." This was a nightmare, and it was beyond both of them as to how the lovely path they had started out on together had become so thorny. Their breakup was more rancorous than either of them could have imagined, with everything under dispute, from child visitation rights to custody of the dog. Bill and Linda were ready to take each other for everything they were worth.

They couldn't bring themselves to cooperate with each other in any phase of the divorce process; the picture of impending financial ruin and emotional turmoil appeared inevitable to both of them. Each had hired an attorney at an expensive rate (she: $200/hour, he: $225/hour), had paid a large retainer, and had been warned that the acrimony of the case could run up astronomical lawyer's fees. Given that their assets totaled $350,000, both knew that the costs of the divorce were wasteful, but the amount of anger and vitriol they were experiencing made them both push for the maximum they could get.

Amy Binder provided research and writing support on this chapter, and Katie Shonk and Leah Kidwell provided editorial assistance.

Each wanted an absolute win for himself or herself and an absolute loss for the other. Mediation, whereby the two parties arrive at a mutual agreement with the help of a trained third party, was out of the question. Adversarial divorce had become the only option. Each one wanted to demolish the other side.

In this situation a dilemma has arisen because each of the parties in the competitive environment (divorce) has pursued a winner-take-all game plan, yet it is in both participants' interest to choose a cooperative strategy and go through mediation instead. Let's look at a slightly less emotional example of this dilemma found in the business world.

You are in charge of pricing for a pharmaceutical firm. Developing a drug often takes years and costs millions of dollars. Many research efforts cost a great deal of money and end up providing no return. Thus, when you find a drug that relieves pain and avoids surgeries, your firm believes in earning as much as possible for its efforts. The main barrier to profitability is competition, which has become fierce. Your most important product is a medicine that prevents second heart attacks. For a number of years, you owned this market, and were selling 10,000,000 pills a year at the rate of $3 per pill. Eighteen months ago, a competitor developed a similar product and has since taken away half of this market. Price competition has nudged the price for each of the two brands down to $2 per pill. Thus, your revenue is down from $30,000,000 (10,000,000 pills at $3 per pill) to $10,000,000 (5,000,000 pills at $2 per pill) and the potential for continued competition to further erode profitability remains.

Your competitor is facing the same problem. Your profits depend not only on the decision you are about to make, but also on the decision your competitor makes. You calculate the various outcomes of your independent decisions. If both companies charge $2 per pill, each obtains a revenue of $10,000,000

(5,000,000 pills at $2 per pill). If both charged $3 per pill, each obtains a revenue of $15,000,000 (5,000,000 pills at $3 per pill). However, if one charged $3 per pill and the other charged $2 per pill, the company that charged $2 per pill would get 90 percent of the market, resulting in the firm with low pricing obtaining $18,000,000 (9,000,000 pills at $2 per pill) in revenue, while the firm with high pricing would only receive $3,000,000 (1,000,000 pills at $3 per pill).

It is impossible for you to discuss this with your competitor. What price will you now charge for one of your pills, $2 or $3? The possible outcomes are summarized in the following table:

| | **You (A)** | |
	$3/pill	$2/pill
Competitor (B) $3/pill	A: $15 million revenue B: $15 million revenue	A: $18 million revenue B: $3 million revenue
Competitor (B) $2/pill	A: $3 million revenue B: $18 million revenue	A: $10 million revenue B: $10 million revenue

Notice that, regardless of what the other side does, you benefit from charging the lower price. If the competitor charges $3 per pill, you would get $15 million if you charged $3 per pill, and $18 million if you charged $2 per pill. If the competitor charges $2 per pill, you would get $3 million if you charged $3 per pill, and $10 million if you charged $2 per pill. Similarly, regardless of what you do, your competitor also benefits from charging a lower price. Thus, both parties in this dilemma possess a dominating strategy to defect by charging the lower price. But if both parties decide to charge the lower price, they both do worse than if both had charged the higher price. While mutually agreeing not to lower prices would be the ideal decision if the two parties were allowed to talk to each other, this option is not viable.

The divorce and the drug scenarios are two examples of the classic Prisoner's Dilemma (more on prisoners later in the chapter). In the divorce story, spending thousands of dollars on legal fees may be beneficial for each side in its attempt to clobber the other side, but when both sides pursue this strategy, only the lawyers benefit. We will look at one more example before thinking more abstractly about how this dilemma causes money mistakes.

Calling All Competitors

The past decade of competition among telecommunications firms for long-distance customers is an intricate situation involving some of the same problems as the divorce and drug scenarios, though it involves a greater number of actors (three instead of just two). After monopolizing long-distance telephone service for decades, telecommunications giant AT&T was ordered by the federal Justice Department in January 1984 to divest itself from its twenty-two Bell operating companies. At the same time, the court ordered local telephone companies to outfit smaller long-distance companies, such as Sprint and MCI, with the local phone connections they required to provide their customers with the same simple dialing access of AT&T. The scene was set for competition in the long-distance market, the likes of which had never been seen before.

Due to the ensuing price wars, consumers were getting good news every month with their long-distance bills. Four years after AT&T's divestment, the average cost of making a long-distance telephone call in the United States had declined by about 38 percent.[1] But using price-slashing to compete with AT&T, which had far greater economies of scale and could support the rate cuts more easily, proved to be an increasing strain on the smaller carriers. At the same time that MCI and Sprint were lowering their rates, they also were spending enormous amounts of cash on improving their systems to match or exceed AT&T's services. This meant that by 1986, big losses were being incurred by both smaller competitors.

Far from surrendering, however, MCI and Sprint became more aggressive in their rate cuts, and especially in *advertising* these cuts. Although suffering losses, Sprint and its owners, GTE Corporation and United Telecommunications, made a commitment to pour money into the enterprise until profits were realized. MCI received a line of credit from IBM, its largest shareholder, for the battle. In 1987, early on in the competition, Sprint and MCI together spent more than $2 billion on marketing and technology, an amount that was only slightly eclipsed by the approximately $2.5 billion AT&T spent to protect its 75 percent market share.[2]

By engaging in a cycle of increasingly untenable rate cuts, the three companies could have done themselves irreparable harm. Nevertheless, the hugely aggressive rate wars won market share for both MCI and Sprint. By 1988, five years after divestiture, AT&T's share of long-distance business had declined to 68 percent of the then $50 billion per year in total profits, with MCI and Sprint at 11 and 7 percent, respectively (many other companies accounted for the remaining 14 percent).[3] While AT&T had expected to lose users, it had not expected to lose so many in such a short amount of time. It did not intend to lose more in the future.

The fierce fight among the three telecommunications providers was on, and it was beginning to look like a street rumble. In 1989 all three companies unleashed a torrent of advertisements bashing each other's rates and engaging in direct comparisons between their services. The combatants were "pit bulls wearing pinstripes," according to one *Advertising Age* article.[4] From 1989 to 1990, for example, AT&T increased its long-distance advertising by about 40 percent, while Sprint raised its spending by nearly 56 percent, and MCI's rose by about 23 percent in the same period.[5]

The three competitors also barraged the public with telephone calls—you know, the ones that try to woo you away from your current long-distance provider during the dinner hour. Most people were annoyed by the calls and would hang up without listening to the sales pitch. Others made a game of it. They would switch for a month or two to take advantage of a spectacular promotion, and then switch back (or over to the third company) two months later for the latest lure. Overall, the three competitors were spending a fortune cycling and recycling customers.

By 1990 it had become clear that consumers were sick and tired of the unprecedented number of long-distance ads. Market share was unaffected, for the three competitors were "still getting the same piece of the bone as when their fighting started."[6] The fast pace of competitors' counteradvertising had nullified the impact of each company's increased advertising spending, and no one firm was able to emerge as the front-runner. They were spending billions of dollars just to walk in place.

Despite the disappointing results, the war continued over the next several years, until consumers could recite a litany of promotional catch-phrases: "Call Me," "Dime-a-Minute," "Nickel-a-Minute," "True" savings, "Friends & Family," and so forth. In one archival search three years ago, it was found that AT&T, MCI, and Sprint had produced more than 2,500 commercials.[7] The spots themselves took on the tone of extremely hostile political advertisements, replete with character assassinations. It had gotten so scurrilous, in fact, that Sprint unveiled an ad in which spokesperson Candice Bergen scolded the company's competitors for their impolite media behavior and then portrayed her corporate benefactor as the one telecommunications giant that did not engage in negative advertising.[8]

The long-distance carriers had fatigued their customers with their various packages, plans, and offers, not to mention the negative tone of their ads. By giving so many incentives to their consumers to switch, the three firms created a monster they did not anticipate: the disloyal customer. If MCI offered a bonus in either dollars or free calling to folks who switched from AT&T, then sure, some million or so customers would snap up the bait. However, as soon as AT&T provided an enticing package to counteract the MCI offer, those same customers would just switch back. The phone companies had created a scenario that helped no one except the customers who actually made money by playing the long-distance craps games and the advertising agencies that were ringing up receipts from their newfound mother lode.

But the more things change, the more they stay the same. "For the Big Three, this is the second generation of price wars," *Adweek* declared in 1996. "They're claiming they know consumers are worn out after a decade of this stuff, and that this is the kinder, gentler, less negative, more-respectful-of-the-brand-and-consumer version. Still, it's not terribly respectful or simple."[9] If there is another full-fledged outbreak of the long-distance wars, then it will be clear that the three biggest carriers learned nothing from their frustrating, unproductive, and lengthy first round.

Beating the Other Party Hurts All Parties

What do the divorce, drug, and telephone scenarios have in common? All three represent versions of the classic Prisoner's Dilemma phenomenon.

Two partners in crime have been caught by the police and are being held and questioned separately. The police believe strongly that, even if neither of the prisoners confesses or squeals on the other, they can convict both suspects on lesser charges and imprison them for two years. However, the authorities really want at least one conviction on the higher charge and offer both prisoners the same deal. If either one of them gives evidence that would lead to the conviction of his or her accomplice on the higher charges, then charges will be dropped against that prisoner and he or she will walk scot-free while the partner gets a ten-year sentence. If both squeal on each other, then they will each get a six-year sentence. For each suspect, then, if his accomplice squeals, he could end up with a 10-year sentence while the partner walks free and clear. What should the prisoners do? The pair of prisoners are in a predicament where they are both better off collectively if they stay silent (that is, if they *cooperate*) than if they both squeal on each other (that is, if they *defect*). Individually, however, each one of the prisoners profits more from defecting, no matter what the other party does.

A quandary arises whenever each party in a competitive environment has a dominating strategy, but it is in the collectivity's best interest not to choose that strategy.[10] These situations are called "prisoner's dilemmas" when they involve just two parties (the divorce and drug examples), and "social dilemmas" when there are more than two actors in the scenario (the long-distance companies case). A simple analysis of the problem suggests that it is rational to defect. Think of the divorcing husband and wife, who each become more contentious as the other person demands more from him or her, or of the phone companies that continually up the ante, thereby causing the other two companies to compete at less and less profitable levels. Each side becomes so intent on winning (and beating the other parties) that *all* parties in the scenario are hurt.

Let's look at the telephone companies' judgments using what we know about social dilemmas. The three companies share a history, in which each one has had repeated opportunities to make its own decisions, observe the managerial decisions of the other two companies, and then make its own subsequent decisions to either cooperate or defect. In this decision-making environment, the three sides do not communicate directly by announcing to each other what their marketing plans are (this would constitute collusion, after all, which is prohibited by law), but rather communicate through their marketing choices whether they intend to cooperate or compete. The industry goes through multiple rounds of these opportunities over several years, which creates at least some impetus for the parties to cooperate in the long run as they must take into account the consequences of their actions for the future. The question these companies must face is how to construct a beneficial long-term competitive strategy.

Robert Axelrod has studied the prisoner's dilemma game as it occurs in multiple rounds to explore how cooperation emerges among parties in continuing dilemmas.[11] He found that one strategy, named *tit for tat*, consistently beat all others over the series of interactions.

Tit for tat was the simplest of all the strategies Axelrod examined, yet it still produced the most favorable outcomes for competitors over the long haul. The first step in the tit for tat strategy is to cooperate and then imitate (once cooperation has failed) every move that the other party makes. Tit for tat works because it creates much more cooperative relationships and mutually advantageous outcomes among competitors than any other strategy that people pursue. Tit for tat expands the pie of available resources instead of shrinking it by developing an *integrative agreement* with as many opponents as possible.

What happens when the divorcing wife acts according to tit for tat? First of all, she does not hire a lawyer until her soon-to-be ex-husband does, and she does not escalate her demands until he starts to do so. Thereafter, she mimics every move he makes. If you subscribe to tit for tat in the drug story, you charge $3 per pill, but if your competitor charges $2 per pill, you immediately match. If they ever move their price up, however, you should quickly follow rather than waiting to gain market share based on a price differential. In the case of the telecommunications companies, you do not offer increasingly less expensive phone packages in the first round, but you do innovate along these lines in the second round if one of the other two telecommunications firms offered lower rates in the first round.

While the simple solution of tit for tat cannot be perfect for all competitions, the logic behind why it does so well is relevant to all competitive environments. Axelrod offers four prescriptions based on tit for tat for people who are making decisions in the midst of ongoing dilemmas. These guidelines apply equally well to people involved in divorce proceedings (who must first decide about child custody, then ownership of property, then investment plans, and so forth) and business managers who must make decisions in the context of a historical relationship with competitors.

1. Do not envy what your competitors are gaining.
2. Do not be the first party to defect.
3. Reciprocate both cooperation and defection.
4. Do not act too cleverly.

People are inclined to judge their own success relative to the success of others. Doing so leads to envy, and in social dilemmas such as the ones we have looked at above, envy is self-destructive. An alternative, and better, set of criteria for judging how well you are doing is to compare your performance to what someone else could be doing in your place. Given the strategies that the other party is pursuing, are you doing as well as possible?

Tit for tat performs well compared to all other social dilemma strategies, but you can never perform *better* over the long haul than your competitors when you use it. Tit for tat always achieves either the same kind of outcome as the competitor for its user or a little worse. The moral is not to be envious of the success the other person or company is having because, over the long term, you need your competitor's success to do well yourself. Remember that your objective is to expand the pie, not fight to the teeth over a diminishing portion of it. This means performing as well as possible over a series of interactions with another party that is also trying to do well. You are not trying to perform better than your competitor in any one round.

Secondly, play nice. Avoid all unnecessary conflict by cooperating with your competitor as long as the other side does. Before becoming the angel you never knew you were, however, a few qualifications are in order. For one, if the ongoing relationship between you and your competitor is not important compared to the immediate gains you will receive if you defect right away, then simply waiting for the other to defect is not the move to make. If you are unlikely to have to work with this person or company again, defecting immediately brings bigger profits to you than staying nice. In addition, if everyone else in the long-term relationship always defects, then you can do no better than also always following their lead. Being nice is one thing, but always playing the stooge is not the road to travel.

In his third prescription, Axelrod recommends that you reciprocate both cooperation and defection, just as in tit for tat you achieve a balance between forgiveness and retaliation. If you unduly punish the other party for defecting by striking back at them for more than their one defection, then you are risking retaliation. On the flip side of the coin, if you do not retaliate in some way for their defection, you risk being exploited. The best forgiveness-retaliation strategy to pursue is context-dependent. If you are in jeopardy of becoming embroiled in continuous mutual retaliation, then a generous amount of forgiveness makes the most sense. However, if your strategy makes you a sitting duck for exploitation, then an excess of forgiveness will only serve to harm you further.

Axelrod's final prescription warns us to keep our cleverness in check. What does he mean by this, and is it not always beneficial to be one step ahead of our competitor in the wiliness department? Actually, no. Your strategy has to be clear if you want the other side to understand your message and respond accordingly. Masking your intentions works in a fixed-pie situation, where you profit as your competitor fares poorly, but in other cases, it does not always benefit you to be so clever. As we have seen, in the prisoner's dilemma (and in the multiparty social dilemma), each side benefits when everyone cooperates. You have to encourage that cooperation by showing your competitors that you will reciprocate any cooperation, but that you are also ready to retaliate in the case of defection. Your actions through tit for tat make these intentions clear.

Tit for tat is so successful because it has room for all four of these prescriptions. It is nice, retaliatory, forgiving, and clear. The nice aspect keeps you away from unneeded conflict. At the same time, you must be ready to retaliate to discourage the other party from maintaining an environment of defection. Because it is forgiving, tit for tat helps reestablish cooperation, and since it is clear, your own actions are understandable to the other party, fostering ongoing cooperation.

It is important to note that the basis of this cooperation is not trust, per se, but rather the stability and longevity of the relationship. There is a difference between trusting someone and having an incentive to maintain the relationship, but whether the parties trust one another or not is less significant than whether the conditions for a stable pattern of cooperation exist.

Conclusion

As we can see from the examples at the beginning of the chapter and the more abstract Axelrod theory that follows, adopting a winner-takes-all strategy can generate consequences that were never intended. When we become fixated on beating the other party at all costs, we make bad decisions and end up sacrificing our own interests as well as those of our competitors.

Let's revisit the telecommunications example one last time, given what we know now about social dilemmas. Each long-distance carrier had the incentive to champion its own package; however, collectively, all the companies were worse off as a result. The untold millions of dollars spent on barraging customers with hostile advertising and annoying telephone calls came at the expense of profitability. Instead of resolving the social dilemma, the three companies only intensified the conflict.

How might long-distance market share have been better divided up? All three parties (AT&T to the greatest extent) would have been better off providing incentives to keep customers, rather than wasting effort on recycling them. While frequent flyer programs have created enormous long-term costs to the airline industry, they have been very effective in locking in customers to one primary airline.[12] AT&T would have been well advised to spend their money to lock in their 75 or 80 percent of the market, rather than trying to buy back the market share that had been lost.

The main message of this chapter is that people frequently make poor decisions in their negotiations because they pursue a winner-takes-all strategy, and they also neglect to see how this is a money mistake that ought to be monitored. This bias was central in creating the very expensive standstill that the phone companies now face. The phone companies were asking the wrong question. They were asking how they could gain market share when they should have been trying to figure out how they could increase their profitability.

Another critical aspect of the beating-the-other-party strategy is that participants in the social dilemma often fail to consider the decisions of their competitors. This bias clearly occurred in the long-distance wars. When AT&T lowers its rates, for example, the company can bet that the other two companies will follow. And when MCI, for example, offers to send a check for $50 to customers who switch over to their service from another carrier, they can bet that the other carrier will respond similarly. If we do not take into account the marketing decisions of the competition, we can understand the logic of marketers at one of the firms deciding that a $50 check will bring in new (or returning) customers. When we consider the decision strategies of the competitors, however, we realize that the other two companies will match the offer and that all three companies will retain the same market share over the long term, resulting in financial loss for all three companies.

If one of the telecommunications companies had held a press conference to say that it was scaling back its promotions and its role in the rates and advertising wars, but that it was determined to match or better any promotion presented, it would have removed the other two companies' incentives to undercut the rates of the others. In my previous writings, I have documented how Lee Iaccoca used such a statement to end a rebate war in the automobile industry and how Robert Crandall sent such a message to United to avoid a bidding war over the potential acquisition of USAir (now USAirways).[13]

The phone companies neglected to think about what their real objective was: to turn a profit. Similarly, the husband and wife at the beginning of the chapter forgot about maximizing their future happiness apart from one another. Instead, in both cases, both parties sought to beat the competition, but in doing so, they both lost. Certainly, long-distance *users* came out ahead, particularly those who scooped up the free goodies given away during the height of the rate wars, and advertising agencies made out like bandits. But the long-distance companies were left spinning their wheels, churning out hundreds upon thousands of ads, and seeing very few positive results.

Advice

When you find yourself caught in a war in which battle after battle ends in a draw or a loss for both sides, it is time to reevaluate what you and your opponents are fighting for. There is a good chance that a cooperative strategy will produce unanticipated financial rewards for both you and your former bitter enemy. But remember, making nice does not mean being a doormat. The best remedy is always a mixture of cooperation and healthy competition.

12

THE MYTHICAL FIXED PIE

"*I* wish I were a millionaire," Joan says to her husband Phil one Sunday afternoon. It's the first warm day of spring in Chicago, and the couple is taking in the sun on their apartment's back porch.

"What's the first thing you'd buy?" Phil asks, looking up from a crossword puzzle.

"Tickets to the opera. A soprano I really admire is going to be a soloist with the Lyric in a few weeks," Joan says, holding up the arts section of the newspaper.

"I think they let bums like you and me into the opera. I'll take you for our anniversary."

"No way. Not this year at least. It's way too expensive." Married just under a year, Phil and Joan are planning to buy a house in the suburbs and start a family within the next few years. In their efforts to save for the future, they recently broke their tradition of dining out on Friday nights, and have enforced other restraints on their entertainment spending.

"There's nothing wrong with splurging on our first anniversary."

"But I don't think we have to spend a lot of money to have fun," Joan says. "I was thinking we could just have a nice evening at home. We could rent a movie, and I could cook dinner."

Katie Shonk provided research and writing support for this chapter, and Leah Kidwell provided editing assistance.

"You mean like we do every Friday night?" Phil says. "I want to wine and dine you a little. Take in the opera, then a nice meal downtown . . ."

"Just think of what a night like that would cost! Not to mention parking—"

"Well, maybe we should compromise," Phil says uncertainly. "Somewhere between a night on the town and the same old thing, there's got to be a happy medium."

"I guess so," Joan says, frowning. "We could go out, but not to the opera and an expensive restaurant. Do you want to go to a play? Something low-budget?"

Phil shrugs. "That would be okay. And then go out for pizza afterwards?"

"I guess so. I'll see what I can find in the theater listings."

On the night of their anniversary, Phil and Joan end up seeing an experimental play at a small theater in their neighborhood and then eating at an inexpensive Italian restaurant down the street. Disappointed by the amateurish, overly long play, they eat their mediocre food in silence.

"Well, there's always next year," Phil says, coaxing a smile out of Joan as they leave the restaurant.

"Where did we go wrong?" Joan says ruefully.

Clearly, Phil and Joan were dissatisfied with the way they celebrated their first anniversary. During their back porch negotiations, something went awry. What mistakes did they make, and how can they ensure that they do not repeat them on their second anniversary?

We engage in negotiations on a daily basis—at work with our coworkers and clients, in our personal lives with our families and friends, and with total strangers in stores or on the street. Imagine a negotiation you were involved in recently. Perhaps you lobbied for a raise at work or bargained for a vintage desk at an antique store, or maybe you and your spouse simply could not agree on where to go on vacation this year. Many of these negotiations affect our finances—our salaries, homes, and purchases. As a result, it is important for anyone concerned about his or her money to take a careful look at how he or she reaches decisions in interactions with other people.

In this chapter, we examine a fundamental bias in negotiator judgment called the "fixed-pie assumption." This bias leads people to be overly competitive and narrow-minded in the context of two-party negotiations at both the individual and organizational level. I provide remedies for correcting these faulty judgments that can be applied to your interactions with others and, more broadly, to the money matters in your life.

Slicing Up the Pie

Researchers have found that people enter negotiations with the assumption that they will be competing for a fixed quantity of resources.[1] They view the ideal outcome of their negotiation as a pie, and believe that they are competing with their opponent for the biggest piece of the pie. In other words, they automatically assume that their interests directly conflict with those of the other party.

A simplified example of the fixed-pie mentality can be seen in the hypothetical story of two sisters who both want the last remaining orange in the house.[2] The sisters squabble over the orange for several minutes before grudgingly deciding to split it in half. As it turns out, both sisters are dissatisfied with the outcome of their negotiation. One needed the peel from a full orange for a cake she was baking, and the other wanted to make orange juice. Obviously, if the sisters had communicated their needs more clearly to each other, they could have shared the orange in a way that satisfied them both. But because they became caught up in a single-issue argument—who gets the orange?—they were unable to reach a mutually beneficial agreement.

Rather than envisioning a pie or an orange, Joan and Phil pictured a clock whose hands would quickly tick away the precious hours of their first anniversary celebration. With the pressure on, each formulated a plan. When Phil's desire to go to the opera and dinner seemed to clash with Joan's desire to cook at home and rent a movie, they assumed their ideas were in direct competition with one another. As politely and kindly as possible, the couple acknowledged this conflict and tried to remedy it, with disappointing results.

The Competitive Spirit

When parties enter a negotiation with the fixed-pie assumption, they often believe that "what's good for the other party must be bad for me" and vice versa. This win-lose assumption is reinforced by salient examples in our daily lives: political elections, athletic competitions, college admissions, and high-profile legal battles covered by the media. Competition over money heightens the contentious quality of a negotiation, as can be seen in debates over salary, the price of a car or house, inheritance, and divorce settlements.

When parties are competing for a distributive issue, for example, victory in a football game or a mayoral election, a me-versus-them spirit is appropriate. Most situations in our lives, however, are not so clear-cut. Often, negotiations are comprised of multiple issues, each of which is valued differently by the various parties. In many cases, parties who think they are competing for the same goal or reward actually have entirely different, yet compatible, visions of a satisfactory outcome. Nevertheless, by holding fast to the fixed-pie assumption, negotiators focus exclusively on one salient issue under contention. This causes tunnel vision; parties ignore relevant information that could provide a mutually beneficial outcome. In the best case, this results in a limiting distributive agreement. In the worst case, it leads to no agreement at all.

Expanding the Pie

While *distribution* occurs when each party tries to claim the entire pie for him- or herself, *integration* becomes possible when parties work together to enlarge the pie of available resources. Research shows that distributive outcomes are usually suboptimal solutions; it is in the best interest of negotiators to explore the complexities of the situation with their partner. I list several creative problem-solving techniques that will help you broaden the scope of your negotiations and develop integrative agreement packages.

Lose the Attitude

Conventional wisdom dictates that the toughest, firmest, and most aggressive party will win any given negotiation by sheer strength. But even in negotiations in which one party is able to intimidate or coerce the other party, the result will invariably be a distributive outcome that is focused on one issue.

Consider the historic Camp David talks of 1978.[3] In their negotiations over control of the Sinai Peninsula, Egypt and Israel both initially took strong stances, believing their interests to be in direct competition with each other. As the negotiations continued, however, the parties realized that they were involved in something more complex than the distributive ownership of a piece of land. It became clear that Israel was primarily interested in security from land and air attacks, whereas sovereignty was of utmost concern to Egypt. Israel returned the Sinai Peninsula to Egypt in exchange for a demilitarized zone and new Israeli air bases. Once they had abandoned their competitive attitudes, negotiators for the two countries were able to arrive at a solution that satisfied them both.

Size Up the Other Party

As seen in the Camp David example, one of the most important steps in a negotiation is recognizing not only your own interests, but those of the other party. By communicating their interests, parties will usually find that there is more than one issue at stake in the negotiation. Keep in mind that this stage of the negotiation is a two-way street. You must not only quiz the other party about their interests, but communicate the relative importance of your own interests.

Phil and Joan were not nearly as contentious in their negotiations over their anniversary plans as the countries in the examples above, or even as argumentative as the two sisters fighting for the orange. In fact, for the sake of marital harmony, they were willing to sacrifice their individual plans and concoct a new plan. Joan was willing to concede to Phil's desire to make the evening special by going out, and Phil was open to more modest entertainment and dining options. Nevertheless, the evening turned out to be less than ideal. By trying too hard to reach a compromise that would please both of them, Joan and Phil reached a solution that pleased neither of them.

Despite their best intentions, Joan and Phil erred by framing their discussion as a win-lose negotiation, and, as a result, they both wound up losing. By assuming a fixed pie in which going out and staying in were in direct competition, Phil and Joan focused too narrowly on the issues under debate, and failed to notice alternatives that would please them both.

Let's imagine what would happen if Phil and Joan had taken the time to understand the motives behind each of their positions, rather than rushing to plan their evening.

"Why is it so important to you that we go out for our anniversary?" Joan asks Phil.

"Well, I know you like to cook, but sometimes I feel guilty that I don't help out more in the kitchen," Phil says. "So I don't want to just do the usual thing."

"But why is it so important to you that we go to the opera *and* have a nice meal?"

"You were the one who wanted to go to the opera. It seemed very important to you."

"Sure, it'd be nice to go, but I don't have my heart set on it," Joan says. "I wouldn't enjoy it because I'd be thinking about how much money we were wasting the whole time."

"So you really want to stay in all night, like we always do?"

"Well, it would be nice to get home early and relax," Joan says.

By communicating their interests to each other, Phil and Joan have added a host of alternative considerations to their negotiation, such as cost, comfort, and the desire to make the night memorable. They are no longer concentrating on a fixed pie in which going out is directly opposed to staying in. In addition, they have expressed the weight that they have given to the different issues. Joan explained that the opera was not as important to her as Phil had originally thought, while Phil revealed that eating at a restaurant is important to him because he does not want Joan to spend their special evening in the kitchen.

Swap Meet

Once parties have communicated their interests, the next step is for both negotiators to make trade-offs on low-priority issues in exchange for concessions on the issues that are most important to them. The most satisfying agreements result from sacrificing issues you care little about while maintaining the integrity of your primary concern. Here is how this stage might work between Phil and Joan.

> "I can see your point about wanting to do something a little different," Joan says. "I don't want to go to the opera, though."
>
> "Believe me, I don't have my heart set on it," Phil says, laughing, "but I think we should eat out. Then we wouldn't have all those dishes to do after dinner."
>
> "That's true," Joan says. "How about if we go out somewhere nice and then come home and put a movie in the VCR?"
>
> "Sounds like a great date to me."

Because Phil and Joan are a happily married couple who trust each other, it was not difficult for them to make trade-offs on minor issues without compromising the interests most important to them. But what about cases when trust and mutual respect are not ingrained in a relationship between negotiating parties? As we will see in the following example, when parties are suspicious of each other's motives, they will adhere rigidly to the notion of a mythical fixed pie—to their own detriment.

These Buds Are for You

The story of the tiny Czech brewery Budejovicky Budvar butting heads with the mighty American giant Anheuser-Busch inspires comparisons to David battling Goliath—the brave underdog vanquishing the intimidating giant. But when we look closely at this conflict, the issues become more complicated. Was the Czech brewer correct in framing itself as the victim? Was Anheuser-Busch really the aggressor? How did the negotiations between the two parties lead to such a disappointing outcome? As we examine the details of this negotiation, the disappointing outcome appears less inevitable, and new possibilities present themselves.

When Czechoslovakia divided in 1993, the distinctive cultures and heritages of the newly formed Czech Republic and Slovakia flourished after decades of communist oppression. As a result, a growing awareness of the literature, architecture, and (no less important) first-class beer of the Czech Republic developed abroad. The Czech people are fiercely loyal to their ancient microbreweries, which produce some of the best beers in the world, such as Pilsner Urquell, Staropramen, and Budweiser.

Budweiser? Yes, but it is not the Budweiser you are probably thinking of. A lesser known, but by no means inferior Budweiser beer has been brewed for centuries in the southern Czech city of Ceske Budejovice by Budejovicky Budvar, a company that does not want you to confuse its "beer of kings" (16th century Czech royalty adored the brew) with the more common American "king of beers."[4]

In fact, Budvar and Anheuser-Busch have been battling over the Budweiser trademark for the past century. The conflict came to a head with the fall of communism in 1989, when Budvar joined a list of Czech companies clamoring to be privatized by the government and began exporting large quantities of its beer to countries such as Germany and Great Britain. At the same time, Anheuser-Busch set its sights on expansion of the newly opened European market.

Bellying Up to the Bargaining Table

As part of its global sales strategy of forming alliances with international microbreweries, Anheuser-Busch sought an interest in the soon-to-be-privatized Budvar. Immediately, reports of negotiations between Anheuser-Busch and Budvar raised a furor throughout the Czech Republic; citizens feared that the Americans would change the recipe of their great lager and destroy its reputation. Nevertheless, the management team from each party recognized that each could gain a great deal from an agreement and entered negotiations with the goal of discussing two main issues: Anheuser-Busch's desire to purchase a stake in Budvar and the resolution of the Budweiser trademark dispute.

Because both parties acknowledged the presence of two distinct yet overlapping issues, they were ready to embark upon integrative negotiations. Anheuser-Busch promised in writing to "control procedures for the basic brewing process to guarantee the integrity of the Budweiser Budvar brand formulation."[5] In addition, Anheuser-Busch vowed that if it had a stake in Budvar, it would institute wage increases and benefits for Czech workers, a no-layoff guarantee, and open up worldwide access for Budvar.

Negotiations proceeded slowly but steadily. In early 1994, the Czech government revealed that it was prepared to sell Anheuser-Busch a stake of up to 34 percent in Budvar, and in the ensuing months, the two brewers agreed to prolong a moratorium on legal proceedings surrounding the Budweiser trademark.[6] "We discovered that it's better to try to make some agreement than to fight," said one Czech government official.[7] "It's a positive thing," said Budvar director Jiri Bocek in January 1994, "that a trademark agreement and the privatization of Budvar will be worked out at the same time."[8] Anheuser-Busch was equally optimistic: "We believe we have found a way for our two companies to end our differences by creating a strategic business alliance that benefits both companies."[9]

But in the following months, Anheuser-Busch became frustrated as the privatization of Budvar proceeded at a snail's pace. Anheuser-Busch resumed its trademark disputes with Budvar in courts across the world to the great financial disadvantage of the small Czech brewery. Formal negotiations broke down, but Anheuser-Busch was not ready to give up its attempts to win in the court of public opinion. The brewer took out newspaper ads espousing its sincerity, and to give the Czechs a taste of what their cooperation would bring, hosted beer festivals and poured millions of dollars into local schools in Ceske Budejovice, Budvar's hometown. Just two weeks after negotiations stalled, Anheuser-Busch hosted the grand opening of the St. Louis Center—a cultural enrichment facility—on the town's main square.[10]

Despite the American corporation's munificence, the Czechs adopted a no-nonsense approach to further negotiations. When the two brewers met at Anheuser-Busch headquarters in St. Louis in late 1995 to try to break their deadlock, an advisor to Czech Prime Minister Vaclav Klaus presented Budvar's plan to retain exclusive European rights to the Budweiser name and to sell Anheuser-Busch the Bud trademark for an undisclosed price.[11] Anheuser-Busch countered by sidestepping the trademark issue, offering a $230 million settlement that included a 10-year agreement to purchase Czech hops worth $76 million and a $20 million deposit toward future shares in Budvar.[12] Budvar and the Czech agriculture ministry rebuffed the offer, insisting that the actual price tag on such a deal was closer to $1 billion.[13]

In 1996 Anheuser-Busch broke off talks with Budvar completely and limited its dealings with the Czech brewer to their trademark battles in courts across the globe. Meanwhile, burned by its experience with the Americans, the government shunned other foreign companies interested in a share of Budvar and planned a management buyout by Czech investors.[14] Each side bad-mouthed the other to the press. Anheuser-Busch accused Budvar of not offering "a credible, substantive counter-proposal in the last five years,"[15] and Budvar's director lashed out against "classic parasitical behavior on the part of the world's largest brewery."[16]

And so there are still two Budweisers in the world, and the century-old dispute remains unresolved. Name confusion will continue in the nine European countries in which Budvar sells Budweiser and Anheuser-Busch sells Bud. Anheuser-Busch's Bud will continue to be marginalized in the Central and Eastern European market as an American beer that is inferior and more expensive than the "real" Budweiser. In addition, the two companies remain tied up in expensive legal battles over the name Budweiser in countries such as Portugal, Egypt, and Italy.[17]

If we agree that both parties could have reached better outcomes in this conflict, what mistakes prevented them from doing so? Assuming that Anheuser-Busch sincerely intended to preserve the recipe of Czech Budweiser, its errors resulted from the fixed-pie assumption. Because Anheuser-Busch was motivated by potential profits to be reaped in Central Europe, it automatically assumed that a motivation for profit was also the primary concern of Budvar. This belief was reflected in its actions. Anheuser-Busch tried to win over the Czechs by contributing funds to the community of Ceske Budejovice, thereby offering prosperity from the Budweiser name.

But to the Czechs, the battle was not over money or sales, but over a name, and their desire to keep it untainted by foreign influence. Increasing its position in the global marketplace was strictly a secondary issue. By removing Budvar's trademark concerns from the negotiations, Anheuser-Busch made an error in judgment. It failed to recognize and make concessions to the primary issue of the other party. Anheuser-Busch took an integrative negotiation and turned it into a distributive one. To win over the Czech people, Anheuser-Busch should have been willing to hash out the trademark issues foremost in the minds of Czechs through cooperative negotiations instead of through courtroom battles.

Interestingly, Anheuser-Busch could have learned from a similar conflict between a Czech brewery and its new foreign owner that was underway at the same time, a conflict that was resolved much more successfully.

Is the Stein Half Empty or Half Full?

When British brewer Bass plc purchased a 34 percent stake in Prague Breweries in 1994, a public outcry, similar to the one raised against Anheuser-Busch, ensued over the fate of the beloved Staropramen beer. A team of British managers venturing to Prague realized that they had acquired a unique beer of excellent quality, and they began exporting massive amounts of the brew to Britain. Recognizing that the Czechs had no need or desire to acquire a taste for expensive foreign beers, Bass made no attempts to saturate the local market with British ale. The Czech public was appeased by Bass's appreciative attitude and ceased its protests.[18]

Thus began a profitable and trusting partnership between Britain and the Czech Republic. Staropramen has flourished under the new regime. In fact, when comparing the taste of the three most popular Czech beers, a beer connoisseur notes that, ironically, Budvar's Budweiser and the country's most popular beer, Pilsner Urquell, have both suffered slightly in recent years from factory modernization undertaken by Czech management. Only British-run Staropramen's flavor has held strong. The expert attributes this to foreign intervention: "Bass's stated intention to maintain the Czech character of Staropramen at all costs looks sincere. The reason for this, of course, is that Bass has realized that the taste of a typical Czech lager is perfect for the international market right now."[19] Thus, the partnership between Bass and Prague Breweries has been a success because the foreign firm has been able to maximize its profits by preserving the distinctiveness and quality of Staropramen.

How Do You Solve the Mythical Fixed Pie?

Budvar and Anheuser-Busch both entered negotiations with the goal of reaching a mutually beneficial agreement. Negotiations collapsed, however, because Anheuser-Busch failed to thoroughly understand the motivation and goals of the other party, which is a crucial step in abandoning the mythical fixed-pie mentality. To reach its own primary goal of buying a stake in Budvar, Anheuser-Busch should have been willing to keep trademark battles out of the courts and confront them head-on in negotiations with the Czechs. If that were accomplished, Anheuser-Busch might have been able to overcome its Goliath reputation and gain Budvar's trust. By overcoming their limiting mind-set, contentious attitudes, and mistrustfulness, the two beer companies could have capitalized on their individual strengths to create a radical new partnership.

The case of the two Budweisers is a more complicated example of the mythical fixed-pie assumption than Phil and Joan's disagreement over how to spend their first anniversary. Paradoxically, though, complicated issues are more conducive to satisfying, integrative agreements. As the number of issues on the table increases, the variety of trade-offs available to the negotiating parties also multiplies. When you find yourself in the midst of an intricate negotiation, consider yourself lucky, for there may be an infinite number of possibilities for you to expand the pie of available resources.

Advice

How do you find these opportunities to expand the pie and bust up the fixed-pie assumption? There is no one strategy that is perfect for all situations. However, the following five strategies provide a practical tool kit:[20]

1. *Build Trust and Share Information.* The easiest way to bust the fixed-pie assumption is to combine information with the other party. Unfortunately, this is easier said than done. We often do not trust the other side.

2. *Ask Questions.* To find out what you need to create mutually effective trades, ask questions and listen attentively. Your negotiation partner may not answer your questions. However, he or she is more likely to respond if you ask them than if you do not. Before you start the negotiation, assess what information you need from the other side; then ask the questions necessary to collect this information.

3. *Strategically Disclose Information.* What do you do in a negotiation in which no trusting relationship exists and the other party is not answering your questions in a meaningful way? Give away some information! Behaviors in negotiation are often reciprocated. When you scream at people, they tend to scream back. When you apologize to a negotiation opponent, they tend to reciprocate, and when you give them useful information, they tend to return with useful information of their own. This strategy can create the information sharing necessary to create mutually beneficial agreements.

4. *Make Multiple Offers Simultaneously.* Many people make a single proposal to the other side, which is rejected or agreed to too quickly. They end up with no agreement

(continued)

(like the Budweiser story) or a suboptimal agreement (like our newlyweds). Instead, present several options simultaneously that are all acceptable to you. Your opponent's preference will indicate solutions that expand the pie, and make you look more flexible!

5. *Search for Post-Settlement Settlements.* After you find a mutually acceptable agreement, stop and ask whether there is a better solution for *both* sides. This is not an opportunity for one side to gain at the expense of the other, but an opportunity for each side to explore mutually beneficial trades. As Raiffa urges, "we must recognize that a lot of disputes are settled by hard-nosed, positional bargaining. Settled, yes. But efficiently settled? Often not . . . [both sides] quibble about sharing the pie and often fail to realize that perhaps the pie can be jointly enlarged."[21]

By favoring cooperation over competition, you and your negotiation partner will be able to establish the mutual trust necessary to thoughtfully consider each other's goals. Once you have overcome your limiting judgments and biases, the next step will be to discuss the issues on the table carefully and to evaluate their relative importance to each party. At this point, both parties should be ready to make concessions on minor issues while holding fast to their primary goal. In this manner, you will be able to develop an integrative-agreement package that satisfies you both.

Chapter

13

GOING, GOING, GONE

It is a scene marked by drama and intrigue. In a crowded room a set of large photographs of a condominium unit is put on a podium in front of an attentive audience, and a man starts rhythmically speaking, chanting an endless stream of words and numbers. Individual members of the audience communicate their desires through discreet signals as understated as a hand gesture or a slight nod. The whole setting takes on its own language and symbols.

"What do I hear for this lovely seaside luxury condominium?" asks the auctioneer, launching into his rapid-fire commentary on the subtle signals of the potential buyers. "Starting at a bargain of one hundred thousand, one hundred thousand . . . do I hear one fifty, one fifty? One fifty from the gentleman with the fedora. Can I get one seventy-five? One seventy-five to the lady on the aisle. Ladies and gentlemen this residence is a bargain at three hundred thousand. Who is going to give me two hundred, two hundred thousand? Thank you sir. Two hundred thousand from the gentleman in the back row.

The hypnotic flow of the auction spirals as the offers climb higher and higher. The large group of bidders drops down to a handful . . . three, then two, and the price rises and rises. Soon each new

Alex Ooms played a central role in the research and writing of this chapter. Katie Shonk and Leah Kidwell provided editorial assistance.

bid is met with a collective gasp. Finally one bidder drops out and the other emerges victorious. The auctioneer closes the bidding—going once, going twice . . . sold!—and the crowd bursts into applause.

Now let's think for a minute. Why, exactly, does the audience applaud? Because they approve of the purchase? Not likely. Many people in an auction audience do not even know the specifics about what is being sold. Are they applauding the outlandish price? Doubtful. People buy things, often very expensive things, every single day. There is no crowd assembled at the Rolls Royce dealership applauding as someone signs the papers to take possession of his or her new car. No, crowds at auctions applaud for a simple reason. It is a show, a contest, and there is a winner (or at least the illusion of a winner). And as we know, everyone admires a winner.

Auctions, by definition, are competitive. If there is only one bidder it is not an auction, it is a sale. It is competition that sellers are hoping to encourage, and it is this competition that makes auctions interesting. Auctions need to have more than one interested buyer and no set price. The buyer is no longer just purchasing a product, he or she is engaged in a test of will, trying to outdo other participants.

In the 1980s bidding at international art auctions went through the roof. Many observers pointed at a new group of bidders: multimillionaire Japanese businessmen and even companies, buoyed by a rising Japanese economy and the tax advantages of investing in art. In 1987 Vincent van Gogh's *Sunflowers* went for a breathtaking $53 million to Yasuda Fire and Marine Insurance Company, and in 1990 Ryoei Saito, the chairman of a Japanese paper firm, paid nearly $83 million—almost twice the expected price—for a single painting, van Gogh's *Portrait of Dr. Cachet.*[1] Swept by the economic tide, bidders may have overstated their mark. The Japanese boom was financed by extended credit from banks and other lenders. When the economic cycle experienced a downturn, many of these investors and companies offered their art holdings as collateral. The expansive art market soon collapsed. According to the *Nikkei Weekly,* "many borrowers have been unable to repay their debt and the collateral has been seized," and before long, art "held by five leading non-bank financial institutions reached 113.9 billion yen."[2] Without the fervid bidding, many of these paintings are now being offered at between one-third and one-fifth of their peak price, when they sell at all. Today many of the paintings bought in the auction boom of the late 1980s sit in temperature-controlled warehouses while their owners wait for a new influx of bidders once the art market recovers so they can recoup a fraction of the paintings' former cost.

In the early 1990s, with the advent of cellular and personal communication systems technologies, previously worthless bandwidth suddenly became very valuable. With sudden demand placed on airwave licenses that previously had been virtually given away, the Federal Communications Commission (FCC), under pressure to try to realize market value for the bandwidth properties, decided to have a series of auctions. When the bidding cleared in 1995 and 1996, after a total of thirteen auctions, the FCC surpassed all expectations and nearly doubled predictions by raising more than $23 billion.[3]

Many observers credited the high bidding to the FCC's liberal payment terms, which often asked for just 10 percent of the price at purchase with the balance deferred. However, most observers also noted that the market was besieged by a number of smaller companies looking to stake their claim in this highly lucrative market. The number of new bidders may have sent prices higher than they should have been. After one auction set aside for small companies, the *New York Times* wrote, "the companies will need to spend billions of dollars on network construction, operations and marketing—all just to compete with at least four other big wireless companies that are expected in every major market within a few years .... That could make these billion dollar bets hard to cover."[4] This prediction was to come true quickly as one company, Pocket Communications, filed for bankruptcy protection within a year after "winning" 43 licenses for a total of $1.4 billion, while other companies have asked the FCC to reschedule payment terms.[5]

The communications auction fever may have peaked. After the well-publicized difficulties of some buyers, the latest round of auctions for wireless licenses, which ended in early 1997, suffered from low bidding. While government analysts predicted sales totaling $1.8 billion, bidders offered only $13.6 million, less than 1 percent of the expected amount.[6] Although observers offered a number of different reasons for the low totals, including holding the auction before many companies were ready to bid, it appears that some companies now think twice about the success of winning bids.

What Makes It an Auction?

Most people think of auctions as dramatic events, a perception that results from our exposure to the movies and to media coverage of art auctions, such as the multiple auctions of Kennedy possessions. There are, however, numerous types of auctions. Aside from open bidding, there are also silent or sealed auctions. Companies often repurchase their own shares through a Dutch auction. In a Dutch auction, the price starts high, and comes down slowly, until someone agrees to pay that amount, and the auction is over. Some auctions have their own set of rules, such as the Vickrey auction, named after the economist William Vickrey, who received the 1996 Nobel Prize for his work. The Vickrey auction is quite simple. Each bidder makes a sealed bid, with the top bidder winning the prize. However, the highest bidder only pays the price of the second highest bid. In their award speech, the Nobel Committee cited the "socially efficient" effects of the Vickrey auction for particular commendation.[7]

Auctions also appear in a variety of places. Estate auctions are common. Police forces often auction off confiscated property or foreclosed land. Business organizations frequently bid against competitors to hire employees and obtain other valued resources, such as contracts, patents, or other firms. Often, there are several parties involved whose identities may or may not be known to the focal organization, and there is little opportunity for communication between competing parties. In California, 1998 marked the debut of a Power Exchange (PX), a computerized auction house where major utilities and other power producers sell their electricity. Prices vary hourly and are determined by auction a day ahead of time, so customers can plan accordingly and run everything from air conditioners to industrial systems when prices are lowest.[8]

These examples vary from the common to the unique, but you might not realize that a lot of purchases are decisions made under competition or the threat of competition. Many of these can be considered auctions. The most common auctions occur over property. If you have ever made an offer for a piece of property where there were other interested parties, or bid for a used car where the owner hinted about other potential buyers, you have made a decision under competition. Consider the following:

> After searching for months, the house of your dreams suddenly comes on the market. It has everything you want—old-style charm and new appliances and plumbing. It is also close to good schools, and it is a reasonable distance from your workplace. It is also affordable. The list price is actually about $25,000 under what you were afraid you might have to pay, and you figure there is a good chance you can get it for less. After looking at the house twice in

one day, you call the real estate broker and say that you are ready to make a bid. The broker tells you that the seller has already had an offer at list price, from the daughter of an old friend of the family. He then asks if maybe you would like to make a more attractive offer. You pause. Should you make another offer over list price? And if so, by how much should your offer exceed the list price?

Suddenly, the presence of competition has affected your decision. What looked like a bargain might now be very expensive. Will you use up your $25,000 buffer? And if you do make an offer, what should it be? A mere extra $1,000 would probably not be enough to change the result, since the agent mentioned that the seller knows the other bidder personally. You have read the earlier chapters of this book and know that once you raise your bid, it will be harder and harder to extract yourself from the situation. Are you ready to get into a bidding war? What if there is something fundamentally wrong with the house, such as it needing an expensive new heating system? Would you ever forgive yourself if you buy it? What should you do?

People choose to sell through auctions because they believe they will get a higher price, and, in most cases, they have set a floor on the lowest price they will consider. If the item does not get above at least a certain price, they will not sell it (a friend in the audience often provides the illusion that no floor to the auction exists, even when the floor is there). In the case of housing, they will set a floor price (below the asking price) and hope that two or more buyers will get into a bidding war. This is a pretty good deal for the seller. They have a minimum price they will accept, and hopefully some competitive bidding will enable them to get more. The specter of competition raises an important question: At what point does it make sense *not* to win?

Why Do People and Companies Lose in Auctions?

In each of the stories in this chapter, a naive analysis would suggest that the winning bidder would be glad to have won the auction. After all, they would not have made their bid if they did not want to acquire the commodity at the price they bid. However, in many of these scenarios, they are likely to have become the most recent victim of the so-called winner's curse in competitive bidding.[9] The winner's curse in competitive bidding is conceptually related to the winner's curse in negotiation introduced in Chapter 9. In the two-party negotiation setting, the winner's curse results from the failure of the negotiator to consider the perspective of the other negotiator, usually the seller. In competitive bidding, the winner's curse is due to the failure of the winning bidder to consider the implications of having bid higher than a large number of other bidders, all of whom are at the same information disadvantage as the winning bidder, relative to the seller.

A possible reason why you were the highest bidder in the above scenario is because you significantly overestimated the actual value of the commodity being sold.[10] Try the following experiment on your friends or coworkers (the more people the better). Fill a jar with coins, noting the value of the money that you put in the jar. Now auction off the jar, offering to pay the winning bidder in bills to control for penny aversion.[11] The following results are very likely to occur. The average bid will be significantly less than the value of the coins (people are trying to make money), and the winning bid will significantly *exceed* the value of the jar. The winning bidder will have voluntarily offered to pay an amount that is a loss to the bidder and profitable to you. Why would anyone bid more than the true value of the money?

Figure 13.1 graphically depicts what occurred.[12] Curve *E*

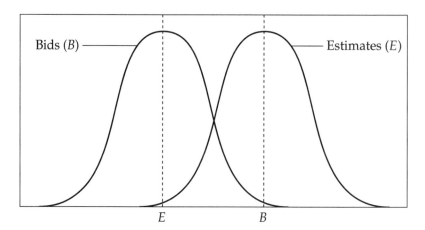

Bids (B) —————— Estimates (E)

E   B

FIGURE 13.1 Graphic illustration of the winner's curse. (From M. H. Bazerman and W. F. Samuelson, "I Won the Auction But Don't Want the Prize," *Journal of Conflict Resolution,* 27(4): 618–634; copyright © 1983 by Sage Publications. Reprinted by permission of Sage Publications, Inc.)

is the distribution of bidder estimates for the true value of the commodity, and curve *B* depicts the distribution of bids. The figure assumes (1) that the mean of the distribution is equal to the true value of the commodity (i.e., no aggregate under- or overestimation is expected), and (2) that bidders discount their estimates a fixed amount in making bids, thereby explaining the leftward shift of the estimate distribution. A winning bid (i.e., one from the right tail of the distribution) is likely to exceed the actual value of the commodity. The highest bidder is likely to have been one of the highest estimators, and unless this bidder had reason to believe that he or she had better information than the other bidders, overpayment can be expected. Bill Samuelson and I argue that the winner in auctions of highly uncertain commodities with a large number of bidders is really a loser. He or she commonly pays more than the commodity is worth.[13]

The winner's curse occurs as a result of the failure of bidders to draw a key inference. If a particular bidder assumes that his or her bid will win the auction, this information should tell the bidder that he or she is likely to have overestimated the value of the commodity in comparison to other bidders. Based on this reasoning, bidders competing against many other bidders for highly uncertain commodities should adjust their estimates downward from the true value of the commodity and lower their bids accordingly. Thus, if they do win, they are less likely to have overbid, or if they have overbid, they have not overbid by the same margin that they would have had no downward adjustment been made.

The likelihood of loss and the magnitude of loss in a competitive bidding situation increase with the number of bidders and the uncertainty of the value of the commodity.[14] Paradoxically, most of us will increase our bids as the number of parties increases. The extra bidders give us more confidence in the worth of the commodity. In concert with our increased confidence, it seems necessary to make a higher bid to beat all the other bidders. However, as more and more bidders enter the auction, the likelihood of at least one bidder being in the extreme right-hand tail of Figure 13.1 goes up. Thus, as the number of bidders increases, there is even more reason to leave the auction. Our intuition tells us just the opposite. Similarly, as the uncertainty of the commodity increases, the range of the bids will increase, again increasing the likelihood of at least one bid being in the far right-hand tail of Figure 13.1. If the value of the commodity was certain, then the bids would fall in a very narrow range. Auctions obviously work best for the seller when the item's value is more subjective and there is therefore a wider distribution of responses (as in Figure 13.1). Bidders fail to incorporate the relevance of the winner's curse and the mediating influences of the number of bidders and commodity uncertainty.

The winner's curse also exists in low-price auctions, in which multiple firms are bidding for a project and the lowest bid wins the contract.[15] In a study by Dyer et al., participants in an auction consisted of a group of construction firm managers who participate in low-bid auctions all the time. The researchers were somewhat concerned that the managers' experience would lead them to make larger profits than is typical of amateurs, but their fears were unfounded. The winner's curse prevailed. The experts did no better than student participants. While these managers may be able to avoid the winner's curse in their specific real-world domain, they lack the expertise to generalize this knowledge to an even slightly different context.

Escalation of Commitment in Auctions

As we saw in Chapter 10, there is a tendency to commit to a course of action and be reluctant to reverse course. Auctions compound this dilemma, because of an additional focus: beating the other bidders. There are numerous examples of auctions where the bidders become so caught up in winning the auction that they overbid for the prize. Winning, not the product, becomes the goal. The escalation of commitment in auctions is not just a problem for individuals; it also affects corporations. In June of 1989, Marvin Davis, the CEO of Paramount Communications, began to consider merger possibilities for his company. Paramount's assets included motion picture productions and distribution, television programming, videocassettes, motion picture theaters, independent and cable television stations, regional theme parks, and Madison Square Garden in New York City. Two bidders were discussed as possibilities: Viacom, with its Chairman Sumner Redstone, and

QVC, headed by CEO Barry Diller. By August 2, Paramount's stock was trading at $52.00 a share; Viacom and QVC were selling for $60.25 and $69.70, respectively.

Davis first tried to engineer a sale to his friend Redstone and the Viacom Corporation. Rumors that the company was for sale quickly drew up the price of its stock. On September 12, Viacom made a friendly takeover bid, offering to buy Paramount's stock, then trading at $61.25, for a price of $69.14 a share. On September 20, knowing that Davis preferred to sell to Viacom and having had their inquires rebuffed, Barry Diller and QVC launched a hostile takeover bid for Paramount with a complicated offer valued at about $80.00 a share. When Davis remained reluctant to consider Diller's offer despite its higher price, QVC filed a lawsuit.

A public bidding war resulted, with a flurry of bids, counterbids, and lawsuits. In late November, a Delaware court ruled that Paramount should give its shareholders the option of choosing the best bid and must therefore consider QVC's offer. Paramount appealed the decision to the Delaware Supreme Court. Both suitors submitted additional bids including cash and stock options. Viacom's offer included a cash price of $85.00 per share, while QVC countered at $90.00. Meanwhile, the stock prices of the suitor companies plummeted as their offers rose. On November 23, prices had fallen to $47.75 per share for Viacom and $48.86 per share for QVC. Fueled by the bidding war, Paramount's stock had climbed to $76.25 per share.

On December 9, Delaware's Supreme Court upheld the earlier ruling and maintained that Davis and the Paramount Board of Directors had to consider the QVC offer. Paramount bowed to the court decision and announced an auction where both Viacom and QVC would submit their best final offers simultaneously in two weeks time. When the smoke cleared, Viacom offered a package including a cash price of $107 per share. QVC's offer, also a mix of options, included a cash price of $104 per share.

The escalation of the bidding war well passed the actual value of Paramount, a fact that was reflected in the companies' share prices. Paramount, the pot of gold at the end of the rainbow, saw its share price climb, not because it became a better company, but simply because anyone holding its shares would receive the cash benefits of the bidding war. The value of the company, as measured by the stock price, increased $3.4 billion in just over six months, from $6.2 billion to $9.6 billion. However, Viacom and QVC, their bidding influenced not only by their desire to acquire Paramount but also by their desire to beat each other, suffered. On February 1, Viacom's stock stood at $39.00 per share, a decrease of 35 percent; QVC fell to $44.75 per share, a decrease of 36 percent. In the end, the Paramount shareholders voted to accept the Viacom offer. Overall, Viacom's loss of market value from the previous August was a staggering $2.6 billion, while QVC had a comparatively modest decline of $940 million.

Did Viacom win in this auction? Not necessarily, according to *Business Week*. In a March 1997 cover story on Chairman Sumner Redstone, *Business Week* noted that the acquisition saddled Viacom with $10 *billion* in debt and caused the price of its stock to drop by half. The end result of the acquisition? "Paying the interest while investing heavily in growth has forced the company into a position where it's actually increasing its debt to fund operations," said *Business Week*.[16] Almost three years later Viacom shareholders still wonder if winning was the right thing.

The reader should note the striking parallels that this story has with the American/United/USAir story described in Chapter 1. Unfortunately, neither of the two suitors for Paramount seemed to be aware of Crandall's effective strategy for averting this dysfunctional bidding war.

Conclusion

Often a buyer may not have the expertise needed to determine what something is worth. In these cases it makes sense to turn to professionals for advice; information from someone knowledgeable in the industry can level the information playing field (see Chapter 9). Many of us are reluctant to pay for a service that we think will only tell us what we already suspect. Remember, though, that what you are buying is not just information, it is an insurance policy on your purchase. The seller limits their downside with a bottom price. As a buyer, you can limit your downside as well.

The auction dilemma can be seen in the context of corporate takeovers. Why do firms pay substantially above market prices to acquire other firms? The popular answer is synergy, but evidence for the existence of synergy does not warrant the premiums that have been paid. Corporate takeovers provide ample evidence that companies often compete against each other to acquire other companies, and they often pay too much for what they get. One-third of all acquisitions prove to be failures; an additional one-third fail to live up to expectations.[17] Research suggests that while stockholders of target firms make significant profits when their firms are purchased, there is no gain to the acquirers.[18]

As a final example, consider baseball teams bidding in the market for free agents. Typically, teams overpay in terms of the true economic worth of the player. The earlier arguments that I used to explain the existence of the winner's curse would lead to the prediction that teams would be most likely to overpay when many teams are bidding and when the teams have diverse opinions about the worth of the player. The owners seemed to have realized the costs of the winner's curse, and they responded with the tactic of collusion. That is, for some period of time, including the 1986–1987 off-season, the teams ceased their bidding on other teams' players. Unfortunately for the team owners, they were subsequently found guilty of illegal collusion and were forced to make restitution to the players. They have since resumed their loss-making competitive bidding practices.

Many managers respond to the ideas in this chapter by arguing that they have to compete in competitive bidding as part of their business. However, we argue that the knowledge from the winner's curse allows managers to select more carefully the situations that warrant a bid, anticipate the impact of many bidders, and realize the value of having accurate information about the worth of the commodity under consideration.

Advice

In auctions, or any decision made under competition, what can you do to try to avoid irrational escalation?

1. Acquire as much information as you can. If you can determine what an item is worth, you will avoid overspending.
2. Above all, know your limits. If you do not have enough information, wait and get some more, and if you think long and hard to establish a top price, stick to it.

Remember, when the applause of the auction is over, you want to make sure you are still happy with the deal.

14

HOW MUCH IS IT
WORTH TO YOU?

Imagine that you bought a painting at an art fair for $50 five years ago.[1] To your great surprise, you recently recognized the artist's face on the cover of a glossy art magazine. Apparently, the former street vendor is now all the rage in SoHo. You visit an art appraiser and learn that your still-life is now worth at least $5,000. Later in the week, you get a call from an art collector who has heard about your find from the appraiser. She offers to buy the painting from you; it's up to you to name your price. When you hesitate, the collector mentions an art opening later in the week and suggests you meet her there. You agree, and promise to tell her the sale price of your painting at the opening. Keeping in mind that you paid $50 for the painting five years ago and that it is now worth approximately $5,000 on the market, write down the minimum amount you would accept for the painting.

Now, imagine that the events of five years ago never occurred (you never bought the street fair painting, etc.). You go to an art opening and see the painting described above. You find yourself immediately attracted to the work. The artist's face is on the cover of

Katie Shonk provided writing and editing support on this chapter, and Leah Kidwell provided editorial assistance.

a glossy art magazine placed near the painting, and the article mentions that his works go for about $5,000. The gallery owner introduces himself to you and questions you about your interest in the painting. Write down the most you would be willing to pay for the painting hanging in the gallery.

Of course, your answers to the two questions in this scenario will depend on your attachment to artwork that you currently own, your interest in collecting artwork, and on the amount of disposable income that you are able to spend on luxury items. But despite these variables, most people will supply answers that follow a distinct pattern. They demand a much higher amount to sell the painting they currently own than they are willing to pay for a very similar painting.

Why is this the case? In this chapter, I argue that our inconsistencies and biases result from a natural tendency to confront specific decisions with blinders on, while ignoring the big picture. One important key to avoiding money mistakes is knowing your objectives (i.e., the value you place on commodities, investments, your time, and so forth). If you do not know where you are going, there are lots of ways to get there. Surprisingly, I have found that many people do not know where they are going. For example, when I ask my students or my friends whether their goal is to die with $10 million in the bank or to die after having spent their last dollar, most people are stumped. While they may have a vague notion of the importance of saving for retirement, they have thought little about the end result of their labor.

Contemplating objectives is a very useful step in thinking through saving versus spending patterns. Not only do we often not think about what we want, we also fail to think through what things are worth to us, and there is ample evidence that we do not have very stable assessments of worth. This chapter explores some of these instabilities in our monetary decisions.

Ownership Effects:
Finders Keepers

The pattern described in the painting example is known as the *endowment effect*, or the tendency of sellers to place a value on their attachment to an item beyond its monetary value.[2] Thus, sellers require a far greater amount to part with an item than they would pay for the item. The endowment effect varies in degree. For example, some of our purchases and acquisitions carry such great sentimental value that they become priceless. Many families, for example, pass antiques down through the generations and would be horrified by the thought of selling them for profit.

However, the endowment effect has been observed even in situations where sentimental attachment is nonexistent. In one experiment by Kahneman, Knetsch, and Thaler, a group of participants, the sellers, were each given a mug and told that they now owned the mug and could sell it to another participant if they liked.[3] Another group of participants, the buyers, were given a sum of money and told that they could keep the money or use it to buy a mug. Sellers charged a median amount of $7.12 for their mug, while buyers were only willing to spend about $3.00 for a mug.

The framing effects of ownership caused sellers to irrationally overvalue the worth of the commodity. We all know of people who have turned down early offers on their house, only to regret their decision after their house gets stuck on the market in the months—and even years—that follow the initial flurry of interest. Often, these sellers have made the mistake of overvaluing the worth of their house.

What can you do to prevent these instabilities from cropping up in your own buying and selling decisions? Following the advice on time in Chapter 5, you should examine the value that you place on a given commodity. Obsessing about getting

193

a fair deal is probably not the best way to maximize your enjoyment in life. Like the novice art collector who is considering unloading his "find" or the husband and wife who are about to sell the home in which they raised their family, you may find it difficult to objectively assess the selling price of something to which you have a strong emotional connection. In such cases, you should seek out an unbiased assessment of the commodity's worth from a knowledgeable but disinterested third party, such as an art, real estate, or jewelry appraiser. Parting with a cherished belonging is difficult enough without the pain of having it rejected over and over again by potential buyers put off by an unrealistically high price.

What a Rip-Off!

Read the following scenario twice.[4] First, read the words in parentheses and exclude the words in brackets. On your second time through the paragraph, read the words in brackets and exclude the words in parentheses. Write down an answer to the concluding question each time you read the story. (If you do not like beer, substitute a nice glass of Chardonnay or a chocolate mocha milkshake).

> You are lying on the beach on a hot day. All you have to drink is ice water. For the last hour you have been thinking about how much you would enjoy a nice cold bottle of your favorite brand of beer. Your companion gets up to go make a phone call and offers to bring back a beer from the only nearby place where beer is sold (a fancy resort hotel) [a small, run-down grocery store]. He says that the beer might be expensive, and asks how much you are willing to pay for a bottle. Your friend says that he will buy the beer if it costs as much as or less than the

price you state. But if it costs more than the price you state, he will not buy it. You trust your friend, and there is no possibility of bargaining with the (bartender) [store owner]. What price do you tell him?

Look at the two figures you've written down. Are they identical? When I present the two versions of the scenario to the left and right side of a classroom, the modal price offered for the resort hotel beer is $5, while the modal price offered for the store beer is $2–3.[5] Why would people refuse to pay $4 for a bottle of beer in one instance and pay $5 for an identical bottle in another situation? There is no difference in the product you receive. You are not receiving any enjoyment from the resort's luxurious atmosphere by buying your beer there because you are going to drink it on the beach. There is no logical reason why people should pay more for the resort hotel beer. So why do they?

Returning to the idea of transactional utility from Chapter 5, paying $5 for a beer from a swanky hotel is an expected annoyance, while paying $5 at a run-down grocery is an outrageous rip-off.[6] No one wants to be considered a sucker. Therefore the terrible grocery store deal becomes more salient to us than the average resort hotel deal. Here we see the irrational focus on transactional utility not just in the context of time, but in the context of how much a commodity is worth.

An overemphasis on transactional utility leads to inconsistent behavior. You might argue that it is your prerogative to be inconsistent—and besides, isn't quibbling over the price of a bottle of beer the worst crime of all? The inconsistent behavior that you exhibit in small-scale purchases, however, is a sign that you are making mistakes in a variety of more important situations. Why not have a consistent way of thinking that will allow you to get more for your money in all areas of your life, both great and small? In the following section, we explore the advantages of confronting financial decisions from a wider perspective than most people typically use.

What's Your Reference Point?

Imagine that you were given 100 shares of stock in XYZ Corporation two years ago, when the value of the stock was $20 per share. Unfortunately, the stock has dropped to $10 per share during the two years that you have held the asset. The corporation is currently drilling for oil in an area that may turn out to be a big hit. On the other hand, they may find nothing. Geological analysis suggests that if they hit, the stock is expected to go back up to $20 per share. If the well is dry, however, the value of the stock will fall to $0 per share. Do you want to sell your stock now for $10 per share?

In reaching your decision, what information from the scenario most caught your attention? Was it the amount of money that you might gain (the amount that you receive for the stock above $0 per share), or was it the amount that you could lose (the amount that the stock has fallen from $20 per share)? Daniel Kahneman and Amos Tversky have shown that how you perceive this problem can have a tremendous impact on your decision.[7] The way a problem is framed, or presented, can dramatically change the perceived neutral point of the question and systematically affect a decision maker's response.

If your anchor is how much the stock was worth, you end up looking at selling the stock as a loss. In contrast, if your anchor is on what you paid—$0—whatever you obtain from the sale is a gain. Decision makers tend to avoid risk concerning gains and seek risk concerning losses. Most people would take a $1,000,000 sure gain over a 50 percent chance of getting a $2,000,000 gain, since the changes to one's life created by $2,000,000 is *not* twice as great as $1,000,000; the first million is more important. In contrast, most people would choose a 50 percent chance of a $2,000,000 loss over a sure loss of $1,000,000, since the negative value placed on $2,000,000 is *not* twice as great as the negative value placed on $1,000,000. The stock market problem can be viewed either as a gain or a loss. If you perceive $0 per share as your reference point, you are likely to be risk averse and take the sure gain by selling the stock now. If your reference point is $20 per share, however, you are more likely to be risk seeking and hold onto the stock rather than accept a sure loss.

Consider the following scenario.

You bought your house in 1992 for $200,000. You currently have the house on the market for $289,900, with a real target of $270,000 (your estimation of the true market value). An offer comes in for $250,000. Does this offer represent a $50,000 gain in comparison with the original purchase price, or a $20,000 loss in comparison with your current target? Objectively, the answer is "both." However, the frame is highly likely to affect your willingness to accept the offer. The $200,000 anchor is much more likely to result in your acceptance of the offer than holding out for the $270,000 anchor.

The same type of framing effect is evident in a corporate negotiation from the summer of 1997, the largest strike in the United States in over a decade. This occurred when United Parcel Service (UPS) drivers who belonged to the Teamsters Union took to the picket lines. A major issue was the wages that UPS paid its part-time workers. While full-timers received approximately $20 per hour, part-timers, often working full-time hours, were getting approximately $8 per hour. Eventually, a proposal was made, with the assistance of the Clinton administration, to raise the part-time wage to approximately $12 per hour over a five-year period.

From the Teamsters Union's point of view, is this a $4 per hour increase over the current part-time pay, or an $8 per hour loss in comparison to the $20 per hour standard wage? For UPS, is this a $4 per hour loss over the current state or an $8 per hour gain in comparison to what full-timers are making? If each side looks at what they have to lose, they are both predicted to be risk seeking and unwilling to take the certain settlement. In contrast, if each side looks at what they have to gain, they are likely to be risk averse and to accept a settlement over the risky option of continuing the strike. Labor and management negotiators with positive frames are significantly more concessionary and successful than their negatively framed counterparts.[8]

Negotiator frame systematically affects negotiation behavior. In one study, my colleagues and I found that negotiators were led to view transactions in terms of either net profit (gains) or expenses (losses) away from the gross profit of the transactions.[9] While both frames yielded the same objective profit result, positively (gain) framed negotiators experienced the risk aversion necessary to have an incentive to compromise. This incentive to compromise led negotiators with a positive frame to complete a larger number of transactions and to obtain greater overall profitability than negotiators with a negative frame.

It is easy to see that the frames of negotiators can result in the difference between an important agreement and impasse. Both sides in negotiations often talk in terms of a certain wage or price that they must get, thereby setting a high reference point against which gains and losses are measured. If this occurs, any compromise below (or above) that reference point represents a loss. This perceived loss leads negotiators to adopt a negative frame toward all compromise proposals, exhibit risk-seeking attitudes, and be less likely to reach settlement.

Framing also has important implications for the tactics

that negotiators use. To induce concessionary behavior in an opponent, a negotiator should always create anchors that lead the opposition to a positive frame, negotiating in terms of what the other side has to gain. In addition, you should make it clear that the opponent is in a risky situation where a sure gain is possible.

Compiling Losses and Gains

Which option is better?

a. Receiving two checks in the mail (on different days) for $100 each.

b. Receiving a single check for $200.

Which option is worse?[10]

c. Receiving a letter from the IRS saying that you made a minor arithmetic mistake in your tax return and must send them $100 and then receiving a similar letter the same day from your state tax authority saying you owe $100 for a similar mistake.

d. Receiving a letter from the IRS saying that you made a minor arithmetic mistake in your tax return and must send them $200.

While options *a* and *b* lead to the same result, a gain of $200, most people say they would get more enjoyment from option *a* than option *b*. We value initial gains from a reference point more highly than we value subsequent gains.[11] As a result, most people value the first $100 gained more than half as much as they value receiving a check for $200. When you receive $100 on two different days, you are likely to evaluate each by the neutral reference point of neither gaining nor losing anything.

Turning to the second half of the problem, which of the two situations would be more upsetting? Most people are more upset by the two small losses than the one larger loss, despite the fact that the two sets of outcomes are equal. Most people value initial losses more negatively than subsequent losses, as evaluated in terms of a neutral reference point. Thus, an initial loss of $100 causes more than 50 percent of the loss in value caused by the $200 loss.

When recruiting a new employee, should you display all the company benefits at once, or let them be seen and evaluated one at a time? Should you give in on a number of issues in a negotiation at once, or let the opposition experience each victory independently? Should a company give its workforce a lot of fringes (bonuses, parties, and so forth) at Christmas, or spread them out throughout the year? If you have several presents for a loved one, should you maximize his or her enjoyment and appreciation by giving him or her all the presents at once, or spread them out over days and weeks? Ample evidence suggests that the recipient's comparatively strong valuation of the initial gain would support giving gifts independently. If each gift were evaluated separately, its value to the receiver would be maximized. Dick Thaler asserts that value is maximized by *not* wrapping "all the Christmas presents in one box."[12]

In contrast, we act as if we lose less value by one large loss than by an identical loss suffered in multiple parts. Thaler argues that one of the things that makes credit cards attractive is that they pool many small losses (debts) into one larger loss. Financial consolidation agencies also use this preference to their advantage by allowing you to pay off "all of your debt, and owe just one payment every month."[13] This transaction often increases your overall debt because of the higher interest rate that goes along with the consolidation, yet the notion of just paying one monthly bill is attractive to many consumers.

Egocentrism and Valuation of Worth

Imagine that you are the sales executive of your company responsible for one-half of the country. You and your counterpart, who is in charge of the other half of the country, are very competitive, particularly at year-end bonus time. This year, you significantly beat your counterpart in terms of sales percentage increases and sales volume, having thereby established your company's position as the industry leader for the first time. Your counterpart, in contrast, obtained higher profits than you by selling at higher prices. Who deserves a bigger bonus?

When people are in this situation, or the millions of similar situations that occur in organizations, they tend to think that the dimension on which they excel is more important. This allows most of us to be among the top half of employees with our jobs—or at least to think that we are in the top half. Our perceptions are biased in a self-serving manner called *egocentrism*.[14] This type of bias is closely related to the positive illusions described in Chapter 6. However, egocentrism focuses specifically on how people, when exposed to the same information, interpret the information in a way that favors themselves. Egocentrism describes our interpretations of events rather than our personality traits.

Even when faced with identical information, individuals perceive a situation in dramatically different ways, depending on their role in the situation. People frequently have the goal of reaching a fair solution. However, assessments of what is fair are often biased by self-interest. We first determine our preference for a certain outcome on the basis of self-interest and then justify this preference on the basis of fairness by changing the importance of attributes affecting what is fair.[15] It is common for all parties in a conflict to suggest viable but self-serving solutions and then to justify them based on abstract fairness criteria. Egocentrism makes every party in a situation believe that it is honestly fair for him or her to have more of a resource than an independent advisor would judge. This occurs not because of a desire to be unfair, but because of our inability to interpret information in an unbiased manner.[16]

Imagine two people writing a book together. The sum of the percentage contribution that each author would attribute to him- or herself will add up to over 100 percent.[17] This is a problem of collaboration. This is also what was found when husbands and wives were asked to estimate the percentage of the household work that each performed.[18] Harris tells the story of the cowinners of the 1923 Nobel Prize for the discovery of insulin.[19] One cowinner, Banting, lost his graciousness in the aftermath of the award. He contended that his partner, Macleod, who was the head of the laboratory, was more of a hindrance than a help. Similarly, in speeches describing the research that led to the discovery, Macleod managed to forget to mention that he had a partner.

In a famous social psychology study, football fans from Princeton and Dartmouth were asked to view a short film of a football game between the two schools.[20] While both sides watched the same film, each side thought the opposing team played more unfairly and engaged in more aggressive and unsportsmanlike conduct. The researchers observed that the two groups of students "saw a different game." In a study of arms control, both sides of the Cold War attributed failure to reach an agreement to the rigidity of the other side.[21] President Reagan told reporters, "We came to Iceland to advance the cause of peace . . . and although we put on the table the most far-reaching arms control proposal in history, the General Secretary rejected it." Russian General Secretary Gorbachev stated on the same day, "I proposed an urgent meeting . . . because we had something to propose . . . the Americans came to this meeting empty handed." Rod Kramer argues that the memoirs of these leaders suggest that these quotes are more than political representations; they reflect the underlying egocentrism of the diplomatic process.[22]

Leigh Thompson and George Loewenstein found egocentrism affected perceptions of what constitutes a fair settlement, and the magnitude of this bias affected the length of a strike in a simulated labor dispute.[23] In a legal negotiation simulation, researchers presented participants with diverse materials (depositions, police reports, doctors' reports, and so forth) from a lawsuit resulting from a collision between an automobile and a motorcycle.[24] People were assigned the role of plaintiff or defendant and attempted to negotiate a settlement. If they were unable to reach agreement, they paid substantial penalties and were told that the amount paid by the plaintiff to the defendant would be determined by an impartial judge who had earlier read exactly the same case materials and reached a judgment. Before they negotiated, participants were asked to predict the judge's ruling. They were told that this estimate would not be communicated to the other party and would not affect the judge's decision, which had already been made. Nevertheless, plaintiffs' predictions of the judge's award amount were substantially higher than those of defendants, and the degree of discrepancy between plaintiff and defendant was a strong predictor of whether they settled the case.

Egocentrism is said to be greater when the favorable outcome that individuals will receive can be attributed to the individual's group, rather than to just the individual.[25] The group allows people to be more comfortable with their egocentrism. They can explain their behavior based on their department's or family's needs, rather than in their own personal needs. As my insightful colleague David Messick has noted, when a football coach quits one job for a better paying job, we do not hear the coach say, "I wanted more money." Rather, we are much more likely to hear him say, "I wanted to insure the financial security of my family." In reality, these are very similar statements.

Advice

Throughout this book, I have highlighted the numerous mistakes we tend to make with our money. However, even in the context of pointing out errors, I have generally assumed that the decision maker knew what he or she wanted. This chapter provides significant evidence that an additional problem is not knowing where you are going and not knowing what you value. We have also seen that what we value is less stable than many people assume.

When you are focusing on a dilemma, stop and consider what the problem might look like from another vantage point. For example, if you are selling your house, stop and consider what you yourself would be willing to pay for the property in today's marketplace. Put yourself in the buyer's shoes; attend open houses of similar properties in your area and compare property tax estimates in the local paper. Such an assessment might lead you to discover that your asking price is unrealistically high.

The value you place on a given outcome differs depending on your frame. Egocentrism can often trick us into thinking that we are being objective, when in reality, the role we play in any situation alters our point of view. Being aware of these biases will cause you to approach your financial matters more rationally and lead to more rewarding outcomes.

15

AVOIDING MONEY MISTAKES IN THE FUTURE

I hope you now see how your behavior directly impacts your
wallet—whether you overpay when you buy a house or
waste a few dollars driving across town to buy an item on sale.
Sometimes, money mistakes can mean the loss of hundreds,
thousands, and even millions of dollars, as we've seen in some
instances. Sometimes, even more money is at stake, as will become evident in the two cases below.

Fool's Gold

Stock market speculation has always been mired in the opinions of a small group of experts, and as a consequence, sometimes suffers from herd mentality. Investors will often rush to
join a growing trend, even when it is based on a very small

Katie Shonk and Leah Kidwell provided editorial assistance with this chapter.

sign. It is not uncommon for shares to rise or fall based almost solely on the comments of one analyst, company official, or government authority. Early in 1997 Federal Reserve Chairman Alan Greenspan's remark that the stock market suffered from "irrational exuberance" caused a brief downward blip in a rising market. Often investors will buy a stock simply because everyone else is buying it, only to receive particularly dismal results.

In 1996 Bre-X, a small Canadian mining company, vaulted to the heights of the stock market. Reports that Bre-X had struck gold in the Bursang region of Indonesia caused its stock to climb from pennies a share to high-flying status on the Toronto Stock Exchange. Early reports from Bre-X valued the find at up to 200 million ounces of gold, or about $70 billion at current prices. Many investors and some analysts jumped on Bre-X's bandwagon so quickly that they failed to closely examine the geological evidence backing up the alleged gold rush.

In March of 1997 one of Bre-X's top geologists died after jumping from a helicopter in an apparent suicide. Although the company claimed its employee had been depressed over personal issues, rumors began to circulate that his death was related to the developing gold mines at Bursang. Sure enough, within a week the company made an announcement that independent testing by the U.S. mining company Freeport-MvMoRan had revealed that there were only "insignificant" amounts of gold at the sight. When the Toronto stock market opened the next day, Bre-X lost nearly $3 billion in market value in less than thirty minutes.

How could so many people believe in something that vaporized overnight? It was not just investors who were fooled; many other companies bought the story as well. Early on, as the gold claim was investigated, a variety of partners began to stake their claim. According to one article, "so many players investigated the field's potential, extracting their own samples, that analysts have likened parts of Bursang to 'Swiss cheese.'"[1] However, none of the other parties—including Bre-X's consultants, other mining companies, financial firms, and the Indonesian government—discovered the erroneous claims about what was once hailed to be the "biggest gold deposit in the world."[2] In hindsight, it became clear that most of the groups—investors, financiers, and the government—expected that all of the other parties had verified the promising results.

You Only Need One

Overvaluing the opinions of others can be an itinerary for disaster, especially when a so-called expert turns out to be less than qualified. Consider the downfall of Barings Bank, aptly chronicled by Stephen Fay in his book *The Collapse of Barings*.[3] Barings, an English bank almost as venerable as the British Empire itself, was brought to its knees by one of its own employees, a trader named Nick Leeson, who single-handedly lost a total of $1.4 billion on currency trading. At the time, it was the biggest loss in the history of financial markets. Facing mounting losses, Leeson had managed to dupe his colleagues and superiors into thinking that his bogus profits were real. Soon a cult of personality surrounded him. Fellow traders marveled at his success (he was described as a "turbo arbitrageur"), and his bosses, swayed by the tremendous amount of money he appeared to be making for the bank, left him unsupervised. Bank officials relied on the cumulative judgments of others in the firm, and failed to probe deeply into Leeson's trades until it was too late. Eventually, Leeson failed to come up with the money to pay his debts, and his accounting practices were revealed to the world as nothing more than an elaborate shell game.

What is remarkable about the collapse of Barings is that Leeson's superiors, who had risen to their positions at the top of one of England's banks based on the strength of their business acumen, never bothered to check out the improbability of Leeson's claimed success. Leeson, who was just 28 years old and lacked a university degree or any theoretical background in finance, executed his trades using devilishly complicated financial instruments called derivatives. Nevertheless, Barings officials believed that he could easily outperform not only his peers and superiors, but the entire banking industry. In fact, just before the collapse, a memo was circulated that stressed how important it was for Barings to make sure that Leeson wasn't poached by one of its competitors.[4]

What looks like a simple mistake to correct in hindsight (i.e., trusting the opinion of one unlikely source) doesn't preclude the possibility of its being repeated. Proving that those who forget the mistakes of history are bound to repeat them, Leeson's folly was overlooked barely a year later when a Japanese trader named Yasuo Hamanaka cost the Sumitomo Bank a total of $1.8 billion in copper transactions.

How did the money mistakes in the Bre-X, Barings, and Sumitomo episodes occur in seemingly rational markets? Many of the culprits have been reviewed in detail earlier in the book. Escalation, vividness, overconfidence, positive illusions, and overweighting momentary impulses all come to mind. When we see other people making money, these money mistakes quickly rear their ugly heads, and we stop thinking rationally. Far too often, a false sense of safety in numbers causes us to follow the herd. This is the final bias of this book, and one of the most important to overcome. When you see others achieving some degree of success, you will be tempted to stop thinking and instead simply mimic what they are doing.

I believe the information in this book will help you to better manage your money in the future. To help organize the insights included, Figure 15.1 provides a wrap-up of the 24 money mistakes covered in this book, along with a brief description of each and references to previous chapters. I hope

1. **Overconfidence.** The tendency to have unwarranted confidence in your judgment. See Chapters 1 and 6.
2. **Being Unprepared.** The tendency to "wing it" when greater preparation is often the key to avoiding money mistakes. See Chapters 1, 2, 3, and 4.
3. **Ignoring the Cognitions of Others.** Failure to consider the perspective of other parties. See Chapters 1, 2, 9, and 13.
4. **Mythical Fixed Pie.** The tendency to assume that if you win, the other side has to lose. See Chapters 1 and 12.
5. **Overweighting Momentary Impulses.** The tendency to overweight momentary impulses that are in contradiction to your long-term interest. See Chapters 1, 4, and 7.
6. **Anchoring.** The tendency to not adjust sufficiently from an initial anchor. See Chapters 1 and 2.
7. **Escalation.** The tendency to escalate commitment to a previous course of action, even when it no longer makes sense. See Chapters 1 and 10.
8. **Focusing on Beating the Other Side.** The tendency to want to beat the other side rather than make a good decision for yourself. See Chapters 1 and 11.
9. **Ignoring Your Alternatives.** Failure to think about your alternatives, resulting in the loss of power that you have from the ability to use these alternatives. See Chapters 1, 2, and 3.
10. **Falling for Vivid Scares.** The tendency to overweight the potential for vivid, yet rare, bad events. See Chapters 1, 3, and 4.
11. **Positive Illusions.** The tendency to possess inappropriately positive assessments of yourself. See Chapters 3, 6, and 14.
12. **Vividness** (related to No. 10). The tendency to overweight vivid information. See Chapters 4 and 6.
13. **Ignoring the Value of Time.** The tendency to exclude the value of your time in making decisions about saving money. See Chapter 5.

(continued)

FIGURE 15.1 Twenty-four money mistakes.

14. **Overweighting Bargains.** The tendency to focus on getting a good deal rather than getting value for what you spend. See Chapters 5 and 14.

15. **Assuming the Deadline Only Affects You.** Failure to realize that when time runs out on you in a negotiation, it is also running out on the other side. See Chapter 5.

16. **Overly Discounting the Future.** The tendency to underweight the effect of your decision on the future. See Chapter 5.

17. **Ignoring the Interests of Agents.** Failure to realize the interests of agents in the negotiation process, causing you to act as if your agent will always act in your best interest. See Chapter 2.

18. **Denying That Random Events Are Random.** The tendency to see patterns in random events and to deny the existence of true chance. See Chapter 6.

19. **Regression to the Mean.** Failure to realize that dramatic outcomes will revert back to their normal mean. See Chapter 6.

20. **Not Realizing the Good Guy, Bad Guy Routine.** The tendency to assume that the good guy is on your side when confronting a good-guy/bad-guy duo from the same company. See Chapter 3.

21. **Being Affected by the Frame of the Problem.** The tendency to be risk averse to problems framed as gains and to be risk seeking to problems framed as losses. See Chapters 8 and 14.

22. **Obsessive Social Comparison Processes.** The tendency to overweight what other people are getting in making your own decisions. See Chapter 8.

23. **Thinking That 50–50 Is Fair.** The tendency to assume that arbitrary 50–50 splits are fair. See Chapter 3.

24. **Following the Herd.** The tendency to assume that if everyone else is doing it, then it must be worth doing. See Chapter 15.

FIGURE 15.1 (*Continued*)

this information will be useful in preventing you from being victimized like the investors and employees involved in the Bre-X, Barings, and Sumitomo debacles.

A Note on Uncertainty

Now that you're armed with all this new knowledge about your potential biases, are you going to avoid all future money mistakes and make decisions that always turn out to your best benefit? The answer is no. Unfortunately, perfection is an impossible standard because uncertainty can never be completely eliminated from your decisions. President Harry Truman wished for a "one-armed economist" because he was tired of experts who constantly said "on the one hand . . . but on the other hand . . ."[5] Truman's wish was impossible to grant, for a good economist would never provide an answer that did not account for the uncertainty of the future.

While stressing that you will never become a flawless decision maker, I do hope that this book provides you with the knowledge necessary to make wise decisions in the face of uncertainty, particularly in everyday monetary dilemmas. Most of us tend to ignore uncertainty, believing that if we work hard enough, we can control the future. In fact, people have a pathological need to "know now" in situations containing inherent doubt about outcomes.[6] By helping you to understand risk, this book enhances your ability to make and evaluate decisions in uncertain situations. You can make better decisions by accepting that uncertainty exists and learning how to think systematically in risky environments. After all, risk is not bad; it is simply unpredictable. As Robyn Dawes has noted, life without uncertainty would be boring.[7] If admission to the best schools and the best jobs was already predetermined, we would never experience the thrill of meeting our goals. Without dreams and challenges, our lives would be empty. It's your decision whether to accept that uncertainty exists or to try to reinvent a more stable world. The former path will lead you to a happier and more successful life; the latter, I believe, is impossible to achieve.

Final Word

Benjamin Franklin's famous quote, "experience is a dear teacher," is often misinterpreted to mean, "experience is the best teacher." Franklin, however, was using *dear* as a synonym for *expensive.* He went on to observe, "yet fools will learn in no other [school]."[8] Dawes argues that learning from experience is dear and that it can even be fatal. The aim of this book is to help you avoid money mistakes in the expensive school of the real world.

Central to the debiasing structure of this book has been the unfreezing-change-refreezing model introduced in Chapter 1. I have tried to (1) get you to "unfreeze" your existing monetary decision-making processes, (2) provide the content necessary for change, and (3) create the conditions that allow the change to "refreeze." I hope this book has unfrozen your present decision-making processes by demonstrating how your judgment systematically deviates from rationality. Content was provided to allow you to change your decision-making processes. Finally, the book outlines the steps that you need to take to refreeze more rational decision processes. An optimistic but naive view of this book would lead me to expect that its readers would immediately eliminate all money mistakes. This view is naive because it is too early to expect the change process to be fully integrated into your behavioral repertoire. The responsibility for refreezing and using the proposed decision-improvement strategies lies with you. Refreezing requires that you vigilantly review your decision-making processes for the 24 money mistakes identified in this book. Lasting improvement in decision making is a complex task that occurs over time through persistent monitoring. It is easier to identify a money mistake while reading a book about money mistakes than it is to identify a money mistake when you are in the middle of a financial crisis.

My goal has been to discuss interesting topics that you have never before considered, and thus to make you think about money in ways that stimulate new questions and problems in your mind. If you found this book interesting, then I think you will walk away from it with enough knowledge to avoid making significant money mistakes in the future.

ENDNOTES

Chapter 1
Do I Hear $5 for a $100 Bill?

1. Although I won this money, I did not keep it. The money either has been used to provide food and beverages for the class from which it was won, or it has immediately been given to charity.
2. Shubik, M. (1971). The dollar auction game: A paradox in non-cooperative behavior and escalation. *Journal of Conflict Resolution, 15,* 109–111.
3. Staw, B. M. (1976). Knee-deep in the big muddy: A study of escalating commitment to a chosen course of action. *Organizational Behavior and Human Performance, 16,* 27–44.
4. Ziemba, S. (1995, November 10). American to United: Avoid bidding war. *Chicago Tribune,* p. B1.
5. Lewin, K. (1947). Group decision and social change. In T. M. Newcomb and E. L. Hartley (eds.), *Readings in Social Psychology.* New York: Holt, Rinehart & Winston.

Chapter 2
Falling in Love with One Rather Than Three, and Other Common House-Buying Mistakes

1. Fisher, R., and Ury, W. (1981). *Getting to Yes.* New York: Houghton-Mifflin.
2. Tversky, A., and Kahneman, D. (1974). Judgment under uncertainty: Heuristics and biases. *Science, 185,* 1124–1131.

3. Northcraft, G. B., and Neale, M. A. (1987). Experts, amateurs, and real estate: An anchoring-and-adjustment perspective on property pricing decisions. *Organizational Behavior and Human Decision Processes, 39,* 228–241.
4. Judd, D. G., and Frew, J. (1986). Real estate brokers, housing prices and the demand for housing. *Urban Studies, 23,* 21–31.
5. Valley, K. L., White, S. B., Neale, M. A., and Bazerman, M. H. (1992). Agents as information brokers: The effects of information disclosure on negotiated outcomes. *Organizational Behavior and Human Decision Processes, 51,* 220–236.

Chapter 3
I Got the Car for Less Than Invoice

1. Sedwick, D. (1996, October 13). How those dealer add-ons can add up. *New York Times,* Section 11, p. 1.
2. Messick, D. M., Bloom, S., Boldizer, J. P., and Samuelson, C. D. (1985). Why we are fairer than others. *Journal of Experimental Social Psychology, 21,* 480–500.
3. Taylor, S. E., and Brown, J. D. (1988). Illusion and well-being: A social psychological perspective. *Psychological Bulletin, 103,* 193–210.
4. Kramer, R. M. (1994). Self-enhancing cognitions and organizational conflict (unpublished paper).
5. Taylor, S. E. (1989). *Positive Illusions.* New York: Basic Books.
6. Taylor, S. E., and Brown, J. D. (1988). Illusion and well-being: A social psychological perspective. *Psychological Bulletin, 103,* 193–210.
7. Death of a salesman (1997, March 8). *The Economist, 342,* 80–107.
8. Taylor, A. (1996, March 4). How to buy a car on the internet. *Fortune, 133(4),* 164–168.
9. Death of a salesman.

Chapter 4
Vivid Scares

1. Simmons, J. (1995, June 2). Car rental insurance? Heed unposted warnings. *Wall Street Journal,* pp. B1, B9.

2. Fowler, D. (1996, December 23). Extended warranties. *Houston Chronicle*, Business Section, p. 1.
3. Who needs an extended warranty? (1991, January). *Consumer Reports, 56*(1), 21–22.
4. Halverson, G. (1996, July 16). Some insurance policies are best left unbought. *The Christian Science Monitor*, Business and Money Section, p. 8.
5. Rock, A. (1997, February). Just say no to the pitches for credit life insurance. *Money*, p. 39.
6. Caruso, G. R. (1997). Why title insurance? Heatherstone Title, Inc. [On-line]. Available: http://www.heatherstone.com/title/page8.html
7. Owner's title insurance (1997). Title One, Inc. [On-line]. Available: http://www.title-1.com/t1/ownersti.html
8. Caruso, Why title insurance?
9. Eldred, G. (1994). *The 106 Common Mistakes Homebuyers Make (and How to Avoid Them)*. New York: John Wiley & Sons, 188–189.
10. Bary, A. (1994, November 21). Lowly titles. *Barron's, 74(47)*, 18.
11. Eldred, *The 106 Common Mistakes Homebuyers Make*, 188–189.
12. Who needs an extended warranty? (1991, January). *Consumer Reports, 56(1)*, 21–22.
13. Ibid.
14. Feeney, S. A. (1997, January 5). With long-term warranties, the fix may already be in. *New York Daily News*, p. 14.
15. Fowler, D. (1996, December 23). Extended warranties. *Houston Chronicle*, Business Section, p. 1.
16. Recio, I. (A. Dunkin, ed.) (1991, February 18). How much warranty does one car need? *Business Week*, p. 139.
17. Alba, J. W., and Marmorstein, H. (1987). The effects of frequency knowledge on consumer decision making. *Journal of Consumer Research, 14*, 14–25.
18. For example, see Kahneman, D., and Tversky, A. (1973). On the psychology of prediction. *Psychological Review, 80*, 237–251.

Chapter 5
Time's Up: How Much Is Your Time Worth?

1. Tversky, A., and Kahneman, D. (1981). The framing of decisions and the rationality of choice. *Science, 211*, 453–458.

2. Thaler, R. (1985). Using mental accounting in a theory of purchasing behavior. *Marketing Science, 4,* 12–13.
3. Loewenstein, G., and Thaler, R. H. (1989). Intertemporal choice. *Journal of Economic Perspectives, 3,* 197–201; Gately, D. (1980). Individual discount rates and the purchase and utilization of energy-using durables. *Bell Journal of Economics, 11,* 373–374.
4. Wade-Benzoni, K. A. (1996). Intergenerational justice: Discounting, reciprocity, and fairness as factors that influence how resources are allocated across generations (Doctoral dissertation, Northwestern University).
5. Herman Daly, cited in Gore, A. (1993). *Earth in the Balance.* New York: Penguin Books USA, p. 191.
6. Bazerman, M. H., Wade-Benzoni, K. A., and Benzoni, F. J. (1996). Environmental degradation: Exploring the rift between environmentally benign attitudes and environmentally destructive behaviors. In D. Messick and A. E. Tenbrunsel (eds.), *Codes of Conduct: Behavioral Research into Business Ethics.* New York: Russell Sage Foundation, pp. 256–274.

Chapter 6
Have I Got a Mutual Fund for You!

1. Hulbert, M. (1993). *Hulbert Guide to Financial Newsletters,* 5th ed. Chicago: Dearborn Financial Publishing Company.
2. Bogle, J. C. (1994). *Bogle on Mutual Funds.* Burr Ridge, Ill.: Irwin.
3. Ibid., p. 89.
4. McGough, R. (1997, April 4). Mutual funds quarterly review: Late slump hits stock funds. *Wall Street Journal,* p. R1.
5. Damato, K. (1997, April 4). Mutual funds quarterly review: Ghosts of dead funds may haunt results. *Wall Street Journal,* p. R1.
6. Ibid.
7. Curran, J. J. (1987). Why investors make the wrong choices. *Fortune (1987 Investor's Guide).*
8. Gilovich, T., Vallone, R., and Tversky, A. (1985). The hot hand in basketball: On the misperception of random sequences. *Cognitive Psychology, 17,* 295–314.
9. Bogle, *Bogle on Mutual Funds.*
10. Kahneman, D., and Tversky, A. (1973). On the psychology of prediction. *Psychological Review, 80,* 237–251.

11. Beardstown Ladies disclose returns were overstated (1998, March). Yeske & Company [On-line]. Available: http:// 209.24.93.167/comment1.htm
12. Tritsch, S. (1998, March). Bull marketing. *Chicago Magazine* [On-line]. Available: http://www.chicagomag.com/text/features/ beards/beards.htm
13. Ibid.
14. Ibid.
15. Coleman, C. (1998, March). Beardstown Ladies add disclaimer that makes returns look 'hooey.' Yeske & Company [On-line]. Available: http://209.24.93.167/comment.htm
16. Tritsch, Bull marketing.
17. Ibid.
18. Coleman, Beardstown Ladies add disclaimer.
19. Ibid.
20. Ibid.
21. Tharp, P. (1998, March). Ladies who hunch take stock. *New York Post* [On-line]. Available: http://nypostonline.com/business/ 145.htm
22. Beardstown Ladies disclose returns were overstated.
23. Kadlec, D. (1998, March 30). Jail the Beardstown Ladies! *Time, 151*(12), 54.
24. Beardstown Ladies disclose returns were overstated.

Chapter 7
Which Job Offer Should I Accept? Negotiating with Yourself and Losing

1. Schelling, T. C. (1984). *Choice and Consequence: Perspectives of an Errant Economist*. Cambridge, Mass: Harvard University Press.
2. Strotz, R. H. (1956). Myopia and inconsistency in dynamic utility maximization. *Review of Economic Studies, 23*, 165–180.
3. Blount, S., and Bazerman, M. H. (1996). The inconsistent evaluation of comparative payoffs in labor supply and bargaining. *Journal of Economic Behavior and Organization, 891*, 1–14.
4. Loewenstein, G. (1996). Out of control: Visceral influences on behavior. *Organizational Behavior and Human Decision Processes, 65 (3)*, 272–292.

5. Sutton, R. I. (1991). Maintaining organizational norms about expressed emotions: The case of bill collectors. *Administrative Science Quarterly, 36*, 245–268; Loewenstein, G. (1996). Out of control: Visceral influences on behavior. *Organizational Behavior and Human Decision Processes, 65* (3), 272–292.
6. Loewenstein, Out of control.
7. Ibid.
8. Shefrin, H., and Thaler, R. H. (1988). The behavioral life-circle hypothesis. *Economic Inquiry, 26*, 609–643.
9. Loewenstein, Out of control.
10. Ibid.
11. Bazerman, M. H., Tenbrunsel, A. E., and Wade-Benzoni, K. A. (1998). Negotiating with yourself and losing: Making decisions with competing internal preferences. *Academy of Management Review, 23*, 225–241.
12. Schelling, *Choice and Consequence.*

Chapter 8
What's Fair and Why Do You Care?

1. Kahneman, D., Knetsch, J. L., and Thaler, R. (1987). Fairness as a constraint on profit seeking: Entitlements in the market. *American Economic Review, 76*, 728–741.
2. Lohr, S. (1991, September 22). Lessons from a hurricane: It pays not to gouge. *New York Times*, p. C1–C2.
3. Ibid.
4. Kahneman, Knetsch, and Thaler, Fairness as a constraint on profit seeking.
5. Guth, W., Schmittberger, R., and Schwarze, B. (1982). An experimental analysis of ultimatum bargaining. *Journal of Economic Behavior and Organization, 3*, 367–388.
6. Kahneman, Knetsch, and Thaler, Fairness as a constant on profit seeking.
7. Salovey, P. (1991). Social comparison processes in envy and jealousy. In J. Suls and T. A. Wills (eds.), *Social Comparison: Contemporary Theory and Research*, Hillsdale, N.J.: Erlbaum, pp. 115–138.

8. Bazerman, M. H., Schroth, H. A., Shah, P. P., Diekman, K. A., and Tenbrunsel, A. E. (1994). The inconsistent role of comparison others and procedural justice in reactions to hypothetical job descriptions: Implications for job acceptance decisions. *Organizational Behavior and Human Decision Processes, 60,* 326–352.

Chapter 9
Putting Yourself in the Other Guy's Shoes

1. Kadlec, D. (1997, June 23). Cable's cool again. *Time, 149(25),* p. 55.
2. Samuelson, W. F., and Bazerman, M. H. (1985). The winner's curse in bilateral negotiations. In V. Smith (ed.), *Research in Experimental Economics, 3.* Greenwich, Conn.: JAI Press, pp. 105–137.
3. Ibid.
4. Akerlof, G. (1970). The market for lemons: Quality uncertainty and the market mechanism. *Quarterly Journal of Economics, 84,* 488–500.
5. Ibid.
6. Ball, S. (1991). Experimental evidence on the bilateral winner's curse (Doctoral dissertation, Northwestern University).
7. Valley, K. L., Moag, J., and Bazerman, M. H. (1998). A matter of trust: Effects of communication on the efficiency and distribution of outcomes. *Journal of Economic Behavior and Organization, 34,* 211–238.
8. Wason, P. C. (1966). On the failure to eliminate hypotheses in a conceptual task. *Quarterly Journal of Experimental Psychology, 12,* 129–140; Bazerman, M. H. (1998). *Judgment in Managerial Decision Making* (4th ed.). New York: John Wiley & Sons.
9. Neale, M. A., and Bazerman, M. H. (1983). The role of perspective taking ability in negotiating under different forms of arbitration. *Industrial and Labor Relations Review, 36,* 378–388.
10. Bazerman, M. H., and Neale, M. A. (1983). Heuristics in negotiation: Limitations to dispute resolution effectiveness. In M .H. Bazerman and R. J. Lewicki (eds.), *Negotiating in Organizations.* Beverly Hills, Calif.: Sage, pp. 51–67.
11. Pruitt, D. (1981). *Negotiation Behavior.* New York: Academic Press.
12. Ball, Experimental evidence on the bilateral winner's curse.

Chapter 10
Knowing When to Quit

1. The opening story was adapted from an account of the Orange County bankruptcy by Jorion, P. (1995). *Big Bets Gone Bad.* San Diego, Calif.: Academic Press.
2. Ibid., p. 160.
3. Ibid., p. 97.
4. Ibid., p. 15.
5. Bazerman, M. H., Giuliano, T., and Appelman, A. (1984). Escalation of commitment in individual and group decision making. *Organizational Behavior and Human Performance, 33,* 141–152; Staw, B. (1976). Knee-deep in the big muddy: A study of escalating commitment to a chosen course of action. *Organizational Behavior and Human Performance, 16,* 27–44.
6. Festinger, L. (1957). *A Theory of Cognitive Dissonance.* Evanston, Ill.: Row, Peterson.
7. Staw, Knee-deep in the big muddy.
8. Jorion, *Big Bets Gone Bad,* p. 14.
9. Ibid., p. 10.
10. Unfortunately for the Orange County Board, all relevant third parties failed them. The SEC did not notify the supervisors that it met with Citron and his assistant to discuss possible improprieties just months prior to the collapse. Standard & Poor's and Moody's gave the OCIP consistently high ratings, and two separate auditing firms failed to question the market risk that Citron assumed year after year. The only serious criticism of Citron came from a biased party, his political opponent, John Moorlach (Jorion, *Big Bets Gone Bad*).
11. Ibid., p. 16.
12. Staw, B. M., and Ross, J. (1980). Commitment in an experimenting society: An experiment on the attribution of leadership from administrative scenarios. *Journal of Applied Psychology, 65,* 249–260.
13. Caldwell, D. F., and O'Reilly, C. A. (1982). Responses to failures: The effects of choices and responsibility on impression management. *Academy of Management Journal, 25,* 121–136.
14. AT&T uses new product line to blunt RBOCs. Telecom Publishing Group [On-line]. Available: http://www.telecommunications.com/tic/focus/jan96.htm
15. Teger, A. I. (1980). *Too Much Invested to Quit: The Psychology of the Escalation of Conflict.* New York: Pergamon Press.

Chapter 11
Playing to Win

1. Sims, C. (1988, October 23). AT&T's competition looking more real. *New York Times*, Section 4, p. 6.
2. Keller, J. J. (1987, March 23). The long-distance wars get hotter. *Business Week*, p. 150.
3. Sims, C. (1989, January 22). AT&T's new call to arms. *New York Times*, Section 3, p. 1.
4. Fitzgerald, K. (1990, October 22). Hello? Is anybody listening? Astonishing amount of advertising bombards consumers, who don't seem to be responding. *Advertising Age*, p. 34.
5. Ibid.
6. Ibid.
7. Goldman, D. (1996, October 21). An illusion of choice. *Adweek*, p. 39.
8. Ibid.
9. Lippert, B. (1996, October 21). No hangups: Phone ads blissfully reach out and clobber someone. *Adweek*, p. 80.
10. Dawes, R. (1988). *Rational Choice in an Uncertain World*. New York: Harcourt Brace Jovanovich.
11. Axelrod, R. (1984). *The Evolution of Co-operation*. New York: Basic Books.
12. Bazerman, M. H. (1998). *Judgment in Managerial Decision Making* (4th ed.). New York: John Wiley & Sons.
13. Ibid.; Bazerman, M. H., and Neale, M. A. (1992). *Negotiating Rationally*. New York: Free Press.

Chapter 12
The Mythical Fixed Pie

1. Bazerman, M. H., and Neale, M. A. (1983). Heuristics in negotiation: Limitations to effective dispute resolutions. In M. H. Bazerman and R. Lewicki (eds.), *Negotiating in Organizations*. Beverly Hills, Calif.: Sage Publications, pp. 51–67; Bazerman, M. H., and Carroll, J. S. (1987). Negotiator cognition. *Organizational Behavior*, 9, 247–288.
2. Fisher, R., and Ury, W. (1981). *Getting to Yes*. Boston: Houghton Mifflin; Follett, M. P. (1940). Constructive conflict. In H. C. Met-

calf and L. Urwick (eds.), *Dynamic Administration: The Collected Papers of Mary Parker Follett*. New York: Harper.

3. Adapted from Pruitt, D. G., and Rubin, J. Z. (1985). *Social Conflict: Escalation, Impasse, and Resolution*. Reading, Mass.: Addison-Wesley.

4. The culture of beer in the Czech lands (1996). Radio Praha web page [On-line]. Available: http://www.radio.cz/beer/beer2.html

5. Cook, J. (1995, September 28). A-B shifts strategy in Budvar bid. *The Guardian*, p. 20.

6. Manor, R. (1992, September 27). One Bud wouldn't change the other, A-B tells Czechs. *St. Louis Dispatch*, p. 1E.

7. Kayal, M. (1994, February 2). Battling breweries' name game nears end. *The Journal of Commerce*, p. 1A.

8. Bloomberg Business News (1994, January 22). But is Spuds' passport current? *The Los Angeles Times*, D1.

9. Czech News Agency (1994, January 21). Budvar negotiates with Anheuser-Busch. *CTK Business News*.

10. Kayal, Battling breweries' name game nears end.

11. Smith, J. (1994, October 11). Separate talks for Budweiser equity and trademark. *Reuters*.

12. Lawson, M. L. (1994, October 26). Battle continues for stake in Czech Budweiser. *The Prague Post*.

13. Mastrini, J. (1995, September 6). Czechs move to settle "Bud" trademark dispute. *The Reuters Business Report*.

14. Boland, V. (1996, December 20). Budvar takes lid off U.S. rival's offer. *Financial Times*, p. 22.

15. Boland, V. (1996, November 1). U.S. brewer leaves Budvar fighting for identity. *Financial Times*, p. 24.

16. Shepherd, R. (1996, January 30). Czech Budvar sell-off plans to go ahead. *Reuters*.

17. Boland, Budvar takes lid off U.S. rival's offer.

18. Czech News Agency (1996, August 21). Anheuser-Busch is far from friendly with Budvar—Budvar CEO. *CTK Business News*.

19. Jefford, A. (1996). Staropramen and Czech lager. Breworld web page [On-line]. Available: http://www.breworld.com/bgbw/jefford4.html

20. Bazerman, M. H., and Neale, M. A. (1992). *Negotiating Rationally*. New York: Free Press; Bazerman, M. H. (1998). *Judgment in Managerial Decision Making* (4th ed.). New York: John Wiley & Sons.

21. Raiffa, H. (1985). Post-settlement settlements. *Negotiation Journal,* 1, 9.

Chapter 13
Going, Going, Gone

1. Montague, B. (1992, March 30). Japan's pricey shopping: Huge deals now look like big mistakes. *USA Today,* p. 1B
2. Art prices fade as stock picture darkens (1993, December 13). *Nikkei Weekly,* p. 24.
3. Marshall, J. (1997, April 21). Economist's auction theory goes to market. *San Francisco Chronicle,* p. C1.
4. Andrews, E. L. (1996, May 7). Big bidders win auction for the small. *New York Times,* p. D1.
5. FCC to rethink plans for wireless payments (1997, June 4). *Chicago Tribune,* Section 3, p. 3.
6. Gruley, B. (1997, June 3). Dollar days: Sale of FCC licenses in several states nets budget pocket change. *Wall Street Journal,* p. A1.
7. Professor William Vickrey. (1996, October 17). *The Daily Telegraph,* Obituary section, p. 31.
8. Marshall, Economist's auction theory goes to market.
9. Bazerman, M. H., and Samuelson, W. F. (1983). I won the auction but don't want the prize. *Journal of Conflict Resolution, 27,* 618–634.
10. Ibid.
11. Thaler, R. H. (1992). The winner's curse. *The Journal of Economic Perspectives, 2,* 191–202. Thaler used the term "penny aversion" in response to individuals not wanting to take home hundreds of pennies.
12. Bazerman and Samuelson, I won the auction but don't want the prize.
13. Ibid.
14. Ibid.
15. Dyer, D., Kagel, J. H., and Levin, D. (1987). The winner's curse in low price auctions. Unpublished manuscript, University of Houston.
16. Lesly, E., G. DeGeorge, and R. Grover (1997, March 3). Sumner's last stand. *BusinessWeek.*

17. Petzinger, T. (1981, September 1). To win a bidding war doesn't insure success of merged companies. *Wall Street Journal*, p. 1.
18. Rappaport, A. (1985). *Creating Shareholder Value*. New York: Free Press, 1986.

Chapter 14
How Much Is It Worth to You?

1. Adapted from Bazerman, M. H. (1998). *Judgment in Managerial Decision Making* (4th ed.). New York: John Wiley & Sons.
2. Kahneman, D., Knetsch J. L., and Thaler, R. (1990). Experimental tests of the endowment effect and the coarse theorem. *Journal of Political Economy*, *98*, 1325–1328.
3. Ibid.
4. Adapted from Thaler, R. (1985). Using mental accounting in a theory of purchasing behavior. *Marketing Science*, *4*, 12–13.
5. Ibid.
6. Ibid.
7. Kahneman, D., and Tversky, A. (1979). Prospect theory: An analysis of decision under risk. *Econometrica*, *47*, 263–291.
8. Neale, M. A., and Bazerman, M. H. (1985). The effects of framing and negotiator overconfidence on bargain behavior. *Academy of Management Journal*, *28*, 34–49.
9. Bazerman, M. H., Magliozzi, T., and Neale, M. A. (1985). The acquisition of an integrative response in a competitive market. *Organizational Behavior and Human Performance*, *34*, 294–313.
10. Adapted from Thaler, Using mental accounting in a theory of purchasing behavior.
11. Kahneman and Tversky, Prospect theory: An analysis of decision under risk.
12. Adapted from Thaler, Using mental accounting in a theory of purchasing behavior.
13. Adapted from Bazerman, *Judgment in Managerial Decision Making*.
14. Babcock, L., Loewenstein, G., Issacharoff, S., and Camerer, C. (1995). Biased judgments of fairness in bargaining. *American Economic Review*, *85*(5), 1337–1343; Babcock, L., and Loewenstein, G.

(1997). Explaining bargaining impasse: The role of self-serving biases. *Journal of Economic Perspectives, 11*; 109–126; Diekmann, K. A., Samuels, S. M., Ross, L., and Bazerman, M. H. (1997). Self-interest and fairness in problems of resource allocation: Allocators versus recipients. *Journal of Personality and Social Psychology, 72(5)*, 1061–1074.

15. Messick, D. M., and Sentis, K. (1983). Fairness, preference, and fairness biases. In D. M. Messick and K. S. Cook (eds.), *Equity Theory: Psychological and Sociological Perspectives.* New York: Praeger, pp. 61–64.

16. Ibid.; Diekmann, Samuels, Ross, and Bazerman, Self-interest and fairness in problems of resource allocation.

17. Taylor, S. E. (1989). *Positive Illusions.* New York: Basic Books.

18. Ross, M., and Sicoly, F. (1979). Egocentric biases in availability and attribution. *Journal of Personality and Social Psychology, 37*, 322–337.

19. Harris, S. (1946). *Banting's Miracle: The Story of the Discovery of Insulin.* Toronto: J. M. Dent and Sons. This story has been retold by many other authors.

20. Hastorf, A. H., and Cantril, H. (1954). They say a game: A case study. *Journal of Abnormal and Social Psychology, 49*, 129–134.

21. Sutton, R., and Kramer, R. M. (1990). Transforming failure into success. Impression management, the Reagan administration, and the Iceland arms control talks. In R. L. Zahn and M. N. Zald (eds.), *Organizations and Nation-States: New Perspectives on Conflict and Co-operation.* San Francisco: Jossey-Bass.

22. Kramer, R. M. (1994). Self-enhancing cognitions and organizational conflict (unpublished paper).

23. Thompson, L., and Loewenstein, G. F. (1992). Egocentric interpretations of fairness and interpersonal conflict. *Organizational Behavior and Human Decision Processes, 51*, 176–197.

24. Babcock, L., Loewenstein, G., Issacharoff, S., and Camerer, C. (1995). Biased judgments of fairness in bargaining. *American Economic Review, 85(5)*, 1337–1343.

25. Diekmann, K. A. (1994). In pursuit of self-interest: The role of fairness and justification in individual versus group allocation decisions (Doctoral dissertation, Northwestern University).

Chapter 15
Avoiding Money Mistakes in the Future

1. Hajari, N. (1997, April 7). Is the pot at the end of the rainbow empty? *Time*, 14.
2. Ibid.
3. Fay, S. (1997). *The Collapse of Barings*. New York: W. W. Norton.
4. Carnegie, M. (1997, March). The story of a young Turk who wanted to make it big. *The American Spectator*, pp. 78–80.
5. Dawes, R. M. (1988). *Rational Choice in an Uncertain World*. New York: Harcourt, Brace and Jovanovich.
6. Ibid.
7. Ibid.
8. Benjamin Franklin quoted in Dawes, *Rational Choice in an Uncertain World*, p. 186.

About the Author

Max H. Bazerman (B.S.E., University of Pennsylvania; M.S., Ph.D., Carnegie-Mellon University) taught at the Sloan School of Management at MIT, Boston University, and the University of Texas before joining the J. L. Kellogg Graduate School of Management of Northwestern University in 1985. He was named the J. L. Kellogg Distinguished Professor of Dispute Resolution and Organizations in 1989 and, in 1991, became the J. Jay Gerber Distinguished Professor. For 1998–2000, he is the Thomas Henry Carroll Ford Visiting Professor of Business Administration and Marvin Bower Fellow at the Harvard Business School, Harvard University. During 1989–1990, he was a fellow at the Center for Advanced Study in the Behavioral Sciences in Stanford, California. He is founder and director of the Kellogg Environmental Research Center, and is on the board of a number of nonprofit organizations.

Professor Bazerman's research focuses on decision making, negotiation, and the natural environment. He is the author or coauthor of over 100 research articles, and the author, coauthor, or coeditor of nine books, including *Judgment in Managerial Decision Making* (1998, Wiley, now in its fourth edition), *Cognition and Rationality in Negotiation* (1991, Free Press, with M. Neale), and *Negotiating Rationally* (1992, Free Press, with M. Neale). He is a member of the editorial boards of the *Journal of Behavioral Decision Making, American Behavioral Scientist, Administrative Science Quarterly,* and *International Journal of Conflict Management,* and is a member of the international advisory board of the *Negotiation Journal*. He was named the 1992 "Teacher of the Year" by the Executive Masters Program of the Kellogg School. He was profiled by *The Organization Frontier* in 1993 as the leading management expert on the topics of negotiation and decision making. His former doctoral students have accepted professorial positions at leading business schools throughout the United States, including the J. L. Kellogg Graduate School of Management at Northwestern University, the Fuqua School at Duke University, the Johnson School at Cornell University, Stanford University, the Graduate School of Business at the University of Chicago, Notre Dame, Columbia, and the Harvard Business School.

His professional activities include projects with Abbott, Aetna, Alcar, Alcoa, Allstate, Ameritech, Asian Development Bank, Astra Merck, BASF, Bayer, Becton Dickenson, Boston Scientific, *Business Week,* Celtic Insurance, Centel, *Chicago Tribune,* City of Chicago, Deloitte and Touche, Dial, Ernst & Young, First Chicago, Gemini Consulting, General Motors, Harris Bank, Home Depot, Hyatt Hotels, IBM, John Hancock, Johnson & Johnson, Kohler, KPMG, Lucent, The May Company, McKinsey, Merrill Lynch, Monitor, Motorola, National Association of Broadcasters, Rhone Poulenc Rorer, Sara Lee, Siemens, Sprint, Sulzermedica, The Nature Conservancy, Union Bank of Switzerland, Wilson Sporting Goods, Xerox, Young Presidents Organization, and Zurich Insurance. Foreign projects include work in Argentina, Barbados, Belgium, Brazil, Chile, Costa Rica, Ecuador, France, Israel, Malaysia, Peru, the Philippines, Switzerland, and Thailand. Bazerman is also a partner in Think! Inc., an executive training and consulting firm.

Index